Dinsdale
Family History

by Karen Proudler & Pauline Batty

First Published in Great Britain in 2013
by Karen & Graham Proudler
Forge Cottage, Field Farm, Aston Lane, Shardlow
Derbys DE72 2GX

A CIP catalogue record for this book is
available from the British Library.

ISBN: 978-0-9566831-3-7

All dates prior to 1752 are old style unless stated otherwise

Contents

Sources

Census Returns for Collingwood Dinsdale; Census Returns for Edwin Dinsdale (Snr)
Lincolnshire parish registers - births; marriages; burials
Birth Certificates: Edwin Dinsdale (Snr) 1854; Henry Collingwood Dinsdale 1856;
Edwin Dinsdale (Jnr) 1896; Eric Dinsdale/Betty Hodgson; Laura Dinsdale, 1921
Joyce Dinsdale, 1928; Maureen Dinsdale 1931; Joan Mary Cornforth 9 July 1938 (mother Irene Dinsdale);
Peter Staley Dinsdale, 1940; Mary Dinsdale, 1948.
Marriage Certificates: of Collingwood Dinsdale, 1857; Edwin Dinsdale (Snr) 1877;
Edwin Dinsdale and Edith Middleton, 1919; Eric Dinsdale, 1939; Marjorie Eleanor Dinsdale, 1941;
Laura Dinsdale, 1942; Joyce Dinsdale, 1952.
Death Certificates: Anthony O'Connor, 1904; Edwin Dinsdale (Snr), 1928; Edwin Dinsdale (Jnr) 1946; Joyce
Dinsdale, 1972; Laura Dinsdale, 1997; Other Dinsdale Branches in Darlington

ORIGIN OF THE DINSDALE NAME

Believed to be derived from the place names of 'Low Dinsdale' or 'Over Dinsdale' in Durham.

One of the earliest written records where the name occurs was of a Geoffrey Dynnesdale in the year 1496.[1] Register of the Freemen of the City of York (Surtees Soc 96, 102, 1897, 1899).

Other early records show a Robert Dynsdale in 1558 at St Martin's, Ludgate in London, and John Dinsdale 1621 appears on the Subsidy Rolls for York. Yorkshire Archaeological Society 16, 21, 74, 1894, 1897, 1929

FREQUENCY OF THE NAME

	1881	2012	Change
Dinsdale	1,542	2,099	Slight decrease in percentage of population

---

[1] Oxford: A Dictionary of English Surnames, by P.H. Reaney. 1997, page 135.

INTRODUCTION

This booklet is an examination of one branch of Dinsdales from Lincolnshire, starting with the first generation that could be traced, around the mid-1600s in Lincolnshire. From the earliest times they were farmers or agricultural labourers but, as times changed then so did the work. Relocation gradually took place away from the rural pastures to the coal fields of South Yorkshire and, finally, into the towns and working manual or heavy industries. This branch of Dinsdales arrived in Darlington in 1890 where many descendants still live today but branches have spread far and wide.

Altogether this book investigated some 12 generations of Dinsdales and the aim is to give family members, or anyone with an interest in Dinsdales, a picture of this particular Family Tree.

The information in this book has been compiled by Pauline Batty and Karen Proudler; Pauline is a grand-daughter and Karen's husband Graham is a grandson of Edwin and Edith.

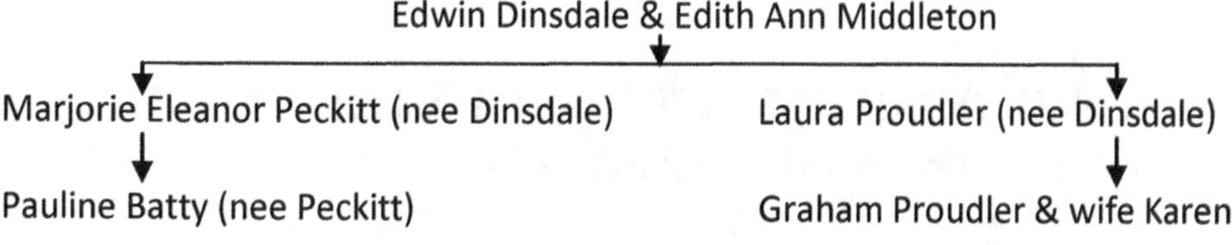

Acknowledgements

This book has been compiled from a variety of sources, including public records and, most importantly, the input of family members with most branches of the family being consulted. Both authors wish to thank everyone who has contributed with photographs, stories and information that has enabled us to piece the family history together.

Acknowledgement also to Richard Dinsdale for sharing his research and the Lincolnshire Family History Society for loan of microfiche of original parish registers.

THE DINSDALE FAMILY TREE

Thomas DINSDALE c. 1660-1724
married Katherine Bell at Roxby-cum-Risby, Lincs

Joseph DINSDALE 1689-1721, baptised Roxby-cum-Risby, Lincs
married Ann in Whitton

John DINSDALE 1719-1762, born Whitton, Lincs
married Jane Walker

Joseph DINSDALE 1751-1806, born Whitton, Lincs
married Mary DRIFFIELD

James DINSDALE 1785-1834, born Whitton, Lincs
married to Lydia COLLINGWOOD

Collingwood DINSDALE 1828-1911, born Roxby-cum-Risby, Lincs
married Ann Clara SHEARMAN

Edwin DINSDALE (Senior) 1854-1928, born Keelby, Lincs
married Ellen GURNHILL

Edwin DINSDALE (Junior) 1896-1946, born Darlington
married Edith Ann Middleton

Elsie, Laura, Marjorie Eleanor, Maurice, Joyce & Maureen

Edwin Dinsdale[2] 1896-1946

---

[2] Picture courtesy of Moira Hollis (Edwin's grand-daughter)

EARLY DINSDALES IN THE DARLINGTON AREA

Protestant "Protestors" during the English Civil War

At the time of English Civil War, a group of Dinsdales (it is not known which family they connect to) in 1641-2 appear in the House of Commons' Records as "Protestors" ..... "for the maintenance of the Protestant religion for the county palatine of Durham, for the borough of Berwick-upon-Tweed and the parish of Morpeth".[3] But the specific area that these Dinsdales were representing was Whorleton - which is, in fact, only a few miles west of Darlington ..... as the transcript of the document shows below, the Dinsdale men, along with everyone else in the parish, were keen to show their anti-Catholic persuasions and to declare that there were no "Papists" among them: "Anthony Dinsdale, William Dinsdale, John Dinsdale, Christopher Dinsdale, Thomas Dinsdale. Curate of the said Chapelry: Henry Armitage, High Constable: Ambrose Johnson, Churchwarden and overseer for the poor: John Shutt, did take the said protestation before his unities, Justices of Peace, Sr. Lionel Maddison , Sr. George Vaine and Mr. Hugh Wright at Auckland, February the seventeenth, 1641. And all the rest of the said Chapelry did take the said protestation in ye presence of the aforesaid — Henry Armitage, Ambrose Johnson, John Shutt, ye 22 of the same instant, Feb., 1641, according to the directions given from the House of Commons. ' Imps. — Robert Johnson, William Huthert, Anthony Dinsdale, William Dinsdale, John Dinsdale, Christopher Dinsdale, Thomas Dinsdale, John Souleby, jun., Arthure Souleby, John Cockfield, Oswould Souleby, Christopher Heighiey, John Heighley, Anthony Shutt, John Shutt, William Appleby, William Jackson, William Adlard, George Appleby, Thomas Ovington, Robert Bainbridge, Thomas Tayler, James Dent, John Souleby, sen., Francis Shutt, John Shut, jun., William Shutt, William Thomson, Christopher Nelson, William Robinson, George Hewer, John Wilson, Richard Wilson, Thomas Harison, Thomas Huthutt. These are all ye names of all ye men above eighteen years of age so yt we have none yt refuses ye said protestation, for we have no papists in all or Chapelry, neither men nor women. Testes — Curate of **Whorleton**: Henry Armitage, Church warden Overseer: John Shutt, Constable: John Cockfield."

Land Enclosure

Documents, dating from 1705, show William and Robert Dinsdale, and another eight individuals, signing an Article of Agreement for the dividing of Little Newsham Common - north of Whorleton. This was in connection with land which had been owned by the Dowthwaite, Bunny and Bacon families and may well have become available as a result of the Land Enclosure Acts that were being implemented at the time.[4]

MOVEMENT BY COUNTY

Generation 1	Upto 1660	1687-1699		1699-1724	
Lincolnshire	Winterton	Roxby-cum-Risby		Thornton Curtis	
Generation 2	1689-1710	1710-1721			
Generation 3	1719-1762	Whitton, Lincolnshire			
Generation 4	1751-1806	Whitton, Lincolnshire			
Generation 5	1785	1808		1830	
Lincolnshire	Whitton	Roxby-cum-Risby		Haltham-upon-Bain	
Generation 6	1828	1841	1851	1861-71	1881-1901
Lincs/Notts/Derbys	Roxby-cum-Risby	Burnham	Keelby	Letwell	Eckington
Generation 7+	1854-1861	1861-1871	1871	1877	
Lincs/Notts/Derbys/Durham	Keelby	Letwell	Sheffield	Attercliffe	
	1878-1880	1881-1888	1890+		
	Beckingham	Eckington	Darlington		

---

[3] Page 11 of 27. Durham Protestations.

[4] Deeds and family papers relating to property owned by the Dowthwaite, Bunny and Bacon families in Durham and Northumberland. Document dated 23 November 1705, held by Durham University Library, Archives and Special Collections. Reference Code GB-0033-BRA-1260.

THOMAS DINSDALE (circa 1660-1724)

Generation No. 1

THOMAS[1] DINSDALE was born about 1660, and died 1724 in Roxby-Cum-Risby, Lincs. He married KATHERINE BELL 1662-1718 on June 6, 1687 in Roxby-cum- Risby, Lincolnshire. KATHERINE BELL was born in Whitton in 1662 and was buried on 12 August 1718 in Lincolnshire.

Children of THOMAS DINSDALE and KATHERINE BELL are:

    i.   WILLIAM DINSDALE, b. 1687, Roxby-Cum-Risby, Lincs.
    ii.   THOMAS DINSDALE, b. May 19, 1688, Roxby-Cum-Risby, Lincs.
    iii.   JOHN DINSDALE, b. November 10, 1689, Roxby-Cum-Risby, Lincs; d. Bef. 1691, Roxby-Cum-Risby, Lincs.
    iv.   JOSEPH DINSDALE, b. November 10, 1689, Roxby-Cum-Risby, Lincs; d. February 24, 1720/21, Whitton
    v.   JOHN DINSDALE, b. July 1, 1691, Roxby-Cum-Risby, Lincs.
    vi.   THOMAS DINSDALE, b. June 20, 1696, Roxby cum Risby, Lincolnshire.
    vii.   ALICE DINSDALE, b. 1699, Thornton Curtis, Lincs; m. ROBERT CLIFF, 1724, Thornton Curtis, Lincolnshire.
    viii.   SUSANNA DINSDALE, b. 1702, Thornton Curtis, Lincs.

Although the Dinsdale surname is considered to be of Yorkshire/Durham origin, in fact our particular branch is present in Durham today but the origins, as far back as we can trace them, are in Lincolnshire.

It is likely that first generation Thomas Dinsdale belonged to the Whitton Dinsdales who can be traced to the North Lincolnshire area near the coast on the Humber estuary right back to the mid-1500s when the parish registers begin. The Dinsdale family was present in Whitton and, it is thought, Thomas's wife may have came from that village. However gaps in the records make the precise line of descent difficult to follow continuously.

Thomas's birth is estimated to be about 1660, no baptism record has been found for him. Considering the turmoil of the times into which he was born, that would not be too surprising. In the period of the English Civil War, 1640-1660, some twenty percent of all baptism records are missing - either the registers perished or, simply, that the children were not baptised. Some clergy changed from storing parish registers in traditional wooden boxes to metal ones - in the belief that they would afford their precious records more protection - whereas, in fact, they retained moisture and contributed to the pages becoming damp and perishing.

Marriage Record

1687- Thomas Dinsdale and Katherine Bell

married June 6th 1687 Roxby-cum-Risby

Thomas marries Katherine Bell[5] in the summer of 1687. It was certainly a shotgun wedding as, within days of the ceremony on 6th June, a son William is baptised on the 22nd.

Thomas Dinsdale and Katherine Bell

William	Thomas	John	Joseph	John	Thomas	Alice	Susannah
1687	1688	1689	1689	1691	1696	1699	1702

---

[5] Roxby-cum-Risby Parish Register

It is thought that Katherine Bell may have, herself, originated in the nearby village of Whitton - as there was a Bell family resident there at the time. A Jane Bell marries John Westoby in 1740 at Barton-in-Humber and, under the terms of her husband's subsequent Will[6], their sons are bequeathed lands in Whitton. The Westoby and Dinsdale families would, in the course of time, become well known to each other in Whitton, sitting alongside each other in church - see Church Seating Plan on page 20. There is a marriage, later, in 1842 of William Dinsdale (1814-86) to Esther Westoby and their descendants adopt the Westoby-Dinsdale surname.

The couple have six boys - all baptised at Roxby-cum-Risby and then, by 1699, the family move a short distance eastward to an equally small rural village of Thornton Curtis where two girls were born.

The burian record in the parish register of the 12th Century Church of St Lawrence states, in 1724, Thomas's occupation as 'farmer'[7].

It is thought that their fourth son, Joseph, was the Dinsdale who married a girl from the village of Whitton, thus commencing a 130+ year family connection with that village (Joseph heads up generation number 2).

Burial Records - Thomas and Katherine

1724

Burial of Thomas Dinsdale (farmer) of Thornton Curtis

Burial of Katherine Dinsdale on 12 August 1718 (wife of Thomas) in Lincoln.

---

[6] Account Book for John Westoby - Lincolnshire Archives
[7] Roxby-cum-Risby Parish Register

JOSEPH DINSDALE 1689-1721

Generation No. 2

JOSEPH[2] DINSDALE *(THOMAS[1])* was baptised November 10, 1689 in Roxby-Cum-Risby, Lincs, and was buried February 24, 1721 in Whitton, Lincolnshire. He married ANNE about 1710 in Whitton, Lincs.

Children of JOSEPH DINSDALE and ANNE are:
  i. HANNAH[3] DINSDALE, born October 18, 1710, Whitton, Lincs; baptized 6th day of October in 1720 and buried April 6, 1723, Whitton, Lincs.
  ii. JOSEPH DINSDALE, born July 4, 1711, Whitton, Lincs; baptised 1720, Whitton, Lincs.
  iii. THOMAS DINSDALE, baptised March 9, 1719, Whitton, Lincs; buried. March 13, 1719, Whitton, Lincs.
  iv. ALICE DINSDALE, baptised. August 13, 1719, Whitton, Lincs; buried August 14, 1719, Whitton, Lincs.
  v. DINA DINSDALE, baptised August 14, 1719, Whitton, Lincs; buried December 10, 1728, Whitton, Lincs.
  vi. JOHN DINSDALE, baptised August 14, 1719, Whitton, Lincs; d. October 29, 1762, Whitton, Lincolnshire.

Baptism Record

There is a baptism record for Joseph Dinsdale in the Roxby-cum-Risby Parish Register[8]

Baptism of Joseph Dinsdale

10th November 1689 Roxby-cum-Risby

No further record, in the Roxby-cum-Risby parish registers has been found for Joseph but it is believed that he moved the short distance to the village of Whitton where he married about the year 1710 - date calculated from the ages of his various children.

His wife's name was Ann and they had six children, with only one or two surviving to adulthood.

Joseph and Ann

Hannah	Joseph	Thomas	Alice	Dina	John
1710-23	1711-aft 1753	1719-19	1719-19	1719-28	1719-62
Birth date	Birth date	Baptism	Baptism	Baptism	Baptism
(Baptised 1720)	(Baptised 1720)				

This couple did not baptise their children immediately they were born - the records show a glut of baptisms taking place in the 1719-20 period. It seems likely that they were prompted to baptise the children prior to their deaths. Eldest daughter Hannah and son Joseph were not baptised till about the age of 10, but both died within a couple of years. Other children were baptised just a few days before their burials.

Joseph, the father, only lives to 32 years of age and his burial is recorded in the parish register ….

---

[8] Roxby-cum-Risby parish register

Burial Record

1721

Joseph Dinsdaile was buried
February 24

Whitton (Parish Register)

Son John survives to adulthood and he heads up our 3rd Generation.

St John the Baptist Church, Whitton, Lincolnshire

JOHN DINSDALE 1719-1762

Generation No. 3

JOHN[3] DINSDALE *(JOSEPH[2], THOMAS[1])* was baptised August 14, 1719 in Whitton, Lincs, and was buried October 29, 1762 in Whitton, Lincolnshire. He married JANE WALKER (nee Waddingham). She died July 6, 1762 in Whitton, Lincs. 1756 Churchwarden, Whitton, Lincs

Children of JOHN DINSDALE and JANE WALKER are:
- i. ANN[4] DINSDALE, b. Unknown; d. 1746, Whitton, Lincs.
- ii. JAMES DINSDALE
- iii. JOSEPH DINSDALE, b. June 10, 1751, Whitton, Lincolnshire; d. January 23, 1806, Whitton, Lincs

Baptism Record

> *1719*
> *John the son and Dinah the daughter of Joseph Dinsdaill and*
> *Ann his wife was baptised August the 14th 1719…*
> *Whitton Parish Register*

John was baptised in 1719 on the same day as his sister Dinah - who only lived another 9 years; John himself lived to be 43 years old and died in 1762. In the records of the Lincolnshire Marriage Bonds and Allegations (1628-1837, page 402), the following record has been found which contains quite a bit of information on both John and Jane.

Marriage Record

> *1743*
> *Dinsdale, John - Single - not of this Parish intending to marry in the*
> *parishes of Saxby or Horkstow, to Jane Walker - widow - not of this*
> *parish (Ref: MB 1743/111)*

The above entry reveals the surname and marital status of John and Jane (widow) and from this it has been possible to identify Jane as being born as Jane Waddingham of Whitton; she then marries a Thomas Walker of Whitton and has 6 children with him. Walker dies in 1742 and, within a year, Jane (now Walker) marries John Dinsdale and they have 3 children.

Jane has six children prior to her Dinsdale marriage and it is believed that some of her Walker family were instrumental in assisting to raise some of her children from her second Dinsdale marriage after both Jane and husband John die in 1762. Jane was just 49 years old when she died and had given birth to nine children.

Wherever in Lincoln they marry, the couple is in Whitton, certainly by 1746, when the death of a daughter Ann appears in the parish register on 16th February. There is also, in the register, reference to a John Dinsdale, in 1756, being the Churchwarden at Whitton and, from his later burial record, he is referred to as being a labourer.

John dies in his early forties and, although no record of his sons' births have been found, they are mentioned in his 1762 probate record:

> *"Assigned to James Dinsdale and Joseph Dinsdale, minors,*
> *the natural and lawful sons and next of kin of John Dinsdale, late of Whitton*
> *aforesaid, deceased.*
> *Dec ye 29, 1762*

Death of John and Jane

Husband and wife die within three months of each other, as Whitton Parish Register records the following:-

1762
Burial of Jane, wife of Jn Dinsdale - July 6th

1762
Burial of John Dinsdale, October 29th

JOSEPH DINSDALE 1751-1806

Generation No. 4

JOSEPH[4] DINSDALE *(JOHN[3], JOSEPH[2], THOMAS[1])* was born June 10, 1751 in Whitton, Lincolnshire, and died January 23, 1806 in Whitton, Lincolnshire. He married MARY DRIFFIELD May 17, 1776 in Alkborough, Lincs. She was born 1756, and died 1807. Joseph was baptised 10 Apr 1776.
Occupation: Labourer Source: Lincoln parish register - birth and death

Children of JOSEPH DINSDALE and MARY DRIFFIELD are:

    i.   JOHN[5] DINSDALE, b. March 21, 1777, Whitton, Lincolnshire; d. August 26, 1815, Whitton, Lincs.
    ii.   MARY DINSDALE, b. May 15, 1779, Whitton, Lincolnshire; m. RICHARD HILL, May 21, 1804, Whitton, Lincs.
    iii.   EDWARD DINSDALE, b. February 17, 1780, Whitton, Lincolnshire; d. January 17, 1782, Whitton, Lincs.
    iv.   SAMUEL DINSDALE, b. June 15, 1782, Whitton, Lincolnshire; d. August 13, 1841, Whitton, Lincolnshire.
    v.   DINAH DINSDALE, b. August 9, 1783, Whitton, Lincolnshire; d. February 13, 1809, Whitton, Lincs.
    vi.   JAMES DINSDALE, b. April 23, 1785, Whitton, Lincs; d. 1834, East Halton, Lincs.
    vii.   JANE DINSDALE, b. May 5, 1787, Whitton, Lincolnshire; d. August 29, 1810, Whitton, Lincs.
    viii.   ELLEN DINSDALE, b. October 9, 1787.
    ix.   EDWARD DINSDALE, b. July 1789, Whitton, Lincolnshire; d. May 2, 1845, Goxhill, Lincs.
    x.   HANNAH DINSDALE, b. March 5, 1791, Whitton, Lincolnshire; d. March 7, 1792, Whitton, Lincolnshire.
       More About HANNAH DINSDALE: source: Whitton parish register - births and deaths
    xi.   JOSEPH DINSDALE, b. May 11, 1793, Whitton, Lincolnshire; d. April 8, 1873, Glanford Brigg, Lincoln.
    xii.   MARY DINSDALE, b. March 10, 1795, Winterton, Lincolnshire.
       More About MARY DINSDALE:Source: Winterton parish register
    xiii.   RICHARD DINSDALE, b. March 18, 1797, Whitton, Lincs; d. 1851, Lincs.

A little more is known about the next generation, that being Joseph Dinsdale 1751-1806.

Baptism Record

Baptism of Mary, daughter of John and Ann Walker

Baptism of Joseph Dinsdale, aged 25 years, on 10th April 1776

"Baptism - 10th April 1776, Joseph Dinsdale, aged 25 years, not Dinsdale but Dindsdale". See above last two lines.
What is also interesting about the above baptism record is that immediately above Joseph Dinsdale's mature baptism record is an entry for "Mary - daughter of John and Ann Walker". When this 'Walker of Whitton' line is worked back, this is what is found:-

Thomas Walker 1706-1742 m. <u>Jane Waddingham</u> 1713-1762

Elizabeth	Thomas	Hannah	Sarah	**<u>John</u> (m. Ann)**	Hannah
Bap 1735	Bap 1736	Bap 1738	Bap 1739	**<u>Bap 1740</u>**	Bap 1742
Witton	Whitton	Whitton	Whitton	**<u>Whitton</u>**	Whitton

Elizabeth	Dorothy	Hannah	John	Ann	**<u>Mary</u>**	John
Bap 1764	Bap 1766	Bap 1771	Bap 1773	Bap 1774	**<u>Bap 1776</u>**	Bap 1779
Whitton	Whitton	Whitton	Whitton	Whitton	**<u>Whitton</u>**	Whitton

Significance of Jane Walker (nee Waddingham)

So, above, this is the baptism entry that is seen; Mary baptised 1776, daughter of John and Ann Walker. (Ann being Ann Langton[9] who married, on 16 December 1763 Whitton to John Walker [b. 14 December 1740]). Then, John's parents are Thomas and Jane Walker (nee Waddingham). Thomas dies in 1742 and Jane is now widowed.   As there is only one Walker family in the tiny village of Whitton at the time, it is evident that this is the same Walker family that marry into the equally small Dinsdale family. When the now widowed Jane Walker (nee Waddingham) marries, in 1743, to "our" Joseph Dinsdale, they have three children[10]:

John Dinsdale 1719-1762 and Jane Walker (nee Waddingham) 1713-1762

Ann	James	**<u>Joseph</u>**
Born circa 1744	Born circa 1748	**<u>born circa 1751</u>**
Died 1746	Unknown	**<u>died 1806</u>**

All of which means that Joseph Dinsdale (1751-1806) would have been a half brother to John Walker (baptised 1740) in Whitton - both having the same mother but different fathers. When the two surviving Dinsdale offspring from John and Jane Dinsdale do lose their father early, in 1762, it does appear that they have their Walker family to take care of them - hence perhaps Joseph Dinsdale's mature baptism happening at the same time, or very soon after, his half brother's child (Mary's) baptism.

Baptism entry - Whitton Parish Registers 10th May 1776

Joseph Dindsdale, aged 25 years - not Dinsdale but Dindsdale

William Cookson, Vicar

So, from the 'mature baptism' record above, we know his year of birth and this tallies with the age recorded on his gravestone, which has been located - see below page 22.

---

[9] The Langton family, like the Walkers, were also closely associated with the Dinsdales in this small tight-knit community. According to White's Gazetteer of 1842 for Lincoln, William Langton was a farmer in Whitton. The Langtons also sat immediately next to the Dinsdales in Church - see page 21 for Church Seating Plan. Richard Langton was also a church warden, like Joseph Dinsdale.

[10] Walkers were the local shop keepers in Whitton. See 1842 Extract from White's Gazetteer and Directory of Lincoln.

Joseph's family had a history of baptisms taking place later in life: it was probably cheaper for families to baptise more than one child at the same time. There is even, in the Lincolnshire archives, the following:-

The Year 1776

No. 25: Joseph Dinsdale of the Parish of Whitton and Mary Driffield of this Parish were Married in this Church by banns this seventeenth day of May in the Year One Thousand Seven Hundred and Seventy-Six.
By me Robt Storry, Curate of Winteringham.
This Marriage was solemnized between us:
Joseph Dinsdale (signs); Mary Driffield ("X" her mark)
In the Presence of Edward Driffield and Thomas Hills

"John Simpson of Sudbrook, formerly a Quaker. Baptised when 85 years old, in 1828".

The above entry raises another possibility, in that Joseph's family may themselves have been Quakers - as the Quaker movement does not believe in the ritual of baptism. In the case of Joseph, it is perhaps more likely a result of his desire to marry - some vicars would insist that anyone intending to marry in church should be baptised first. Joseph's baptism record appears in the Whitton parish registers and his marriage, just a few days later, in Alkborough. Or, it is possible that Joseph's future wife was a Roman Catholic - when it would have been necessary for him to have been baptised as a Christian in order for the marriage to be considered valid. The marriage record shows him marrying Mary Driffield (1756-1807), who came from Alkborough (next village to Whitton), on 15 April 1776.

Soon after their marriage (see next page) the family is still located in Whitton, where one of their children is born. Whitton is a very small rural village and the family would probably have been employed in farming.

Marriage Record

Joseph and Mary have 13 children, all born in Whitton:-

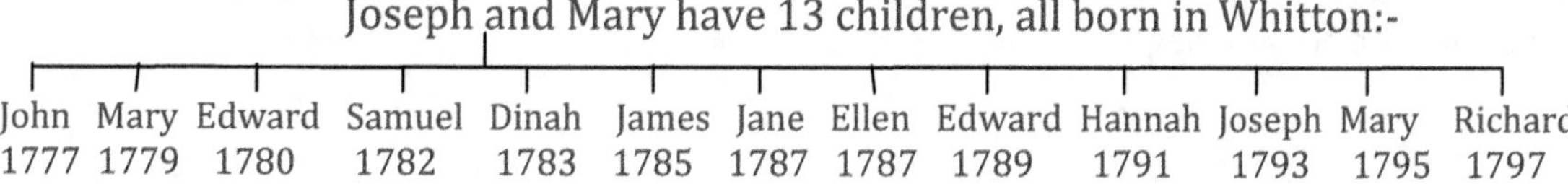

John	Mary	Edward	Samuel	Dinah	James	Jane	Ellen	Edward	Hannah	Joseph	Mary	Richard
1777	1779	1780	1782	1783	1785	1787	1787	1789	1791	1793	1795	1797

Joseph's name occurs again in the 1799 Land Tax Redemption Book (Volume 2); County of Lincoln, Manley Hundred "An assessment in pursuance of an Act of Parliament passed in the 38th year of His Majesty's reign, for granting an Aid to His Majesty by a Land Tax to be raised in Great Britain, for the service of the year 1799".

1799 Land Tax Redemption Records

Name of Proprietor	Name of Occupier	Sums Affected Yearly	Date of Contract
Thomas Goulton Esq	Self	£3-7-4¼	
Thomas Goulton Esq	Joseph Dinsdale	3-¾	

The above record shows that Joseph Dinsdale was a tenant of Thomas Goulton Esq. Thomas Goulton 1745-1826 of Walcot Hall was Lord of the Manor and lessee of the 'great tithes' under the Bishop of Lincoln. During Joseph Dinsdale's life-time, Whitton underwent land enclosure, which was complete by 1775 in that area - where locals would have lost their rights to common land as fences and hedges of quickthorn sprang up over the countryside, and they would have been allocated plots - usually too small to live off, with many being forced into agricultural labour rather than supporting themselves. It is possible that this is how Joseph came to rent land from Goulton. Though, more likely, the Dinsdales had been farming land in this area going right back to the first generation in the mid 1660s, so the land may have been passed through the family to him. The Goulton family had control over Whitton and the surrounding area for some time, with the sister of Thomas - Sarah Goulton - marrying into the Constable family, who became the next generation of land owners.

Writing some 37 years later, in 1836, William Andrew in 'The History of Winterton and the Adjoining Villages' stated that .....

    "Alkborough .... greater part of Lordship belongs to Marmaduke Constable Esq of Walcot Hall."   And ... "Whitton ... the greater part of Whitton is held by the proprietor of the   estates at Walcot and at Alkborough". "The Parish of Whitton is parcel of the Duchy of Lancaster (crown lands) ..... 39 houses and 212 inhabitants.

We have been extremely fortunate that a document has been preserved which records Joseph's involvement with his local church. In 1799 Joseph signed an agreement that was drawn up by, and for, the parishioners of Whitton. Whitton Church had been rebuilt and, in order to avoid disputes over seating arrangements in the church, a plan showing the allocation of pews was devised. Allocation of pews, at that time, was a serious matter and was based strictly on social status with widows being grouped together, another area for female servants, another area for farmers etc etc. The original documents are to be found in the Whitton Parish Registers, but have been reproduced on page 20, they are not good copies but they do contain Joseph Dinsdale's signature, however they have been transcribed as well for clarity on page 21.

MAP OF THE AREA

This is the area of North Lincolnshire where the early Dinsdales were located …

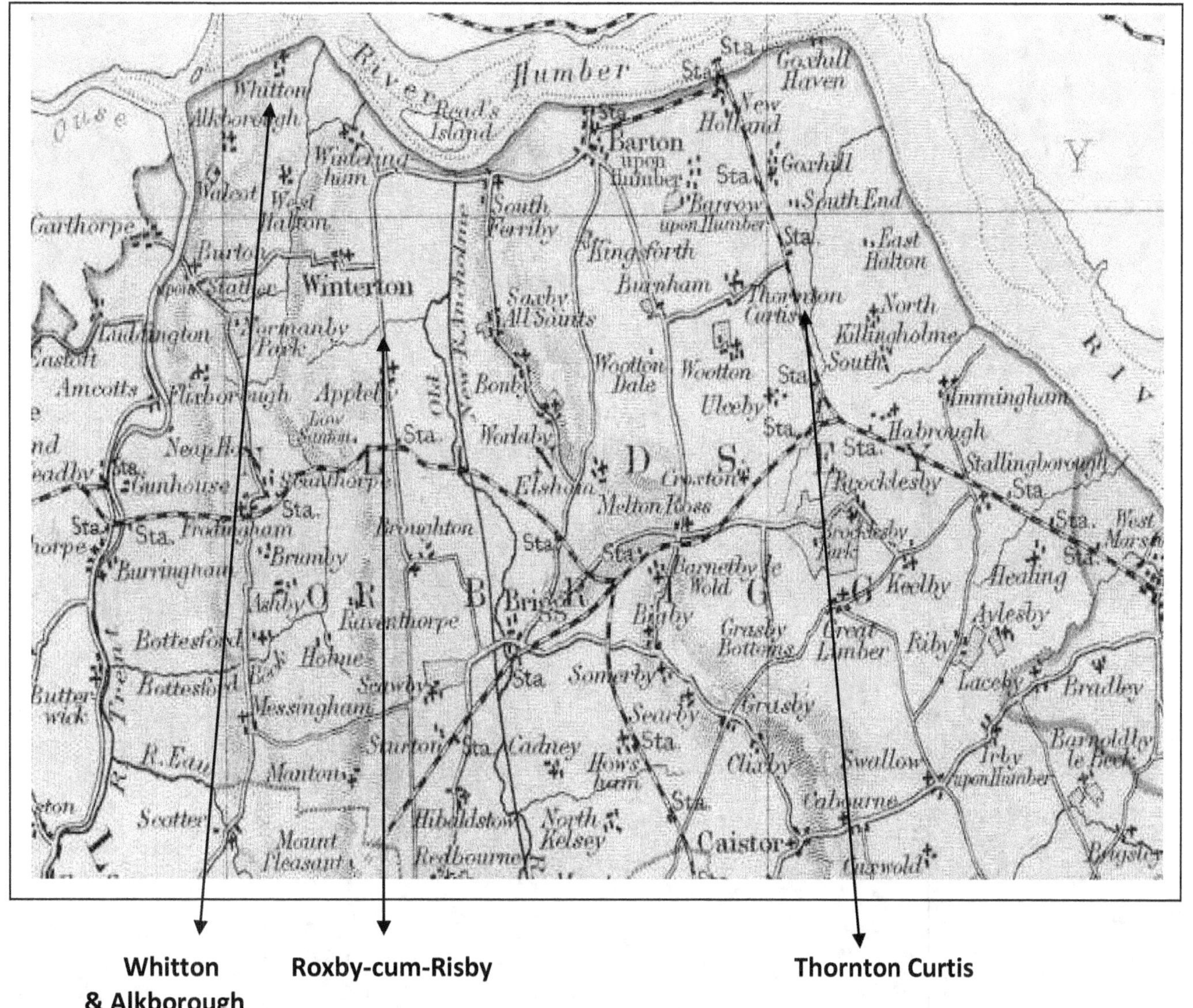

1842 Whitton, an extract from White's '*Gazetteer and Directory of Lincolnshire*'

GREEN John - stonemason,
GREEN Robert - stonemason
LAMMING William - coal merchant
WILSON Rev. John
<u>DINSDALE Joseph - farmer</u>
EVERRATT John - farmer,
Bishopthorpe

MILLSON William - farmer
LEGARD Driffil -farmer
SPILMAN John -farmer, also miller
WILSON Thomas
KENDAL William - shopkeeper
WALKER William - shopkeeper

Seating Plan of 1799 for New Whitton Church, Lincoln[11]

Joseph Dinsdale's signature

Transcript of the above document follows …..

A transcription of the Seating Plan of 1799 for the new Whitton Church

---

Men servants	Men servants
9.Churchwardens Ric'd Langton	8. Vicarage Pew
10. John Walker	7. Saml Butter
11. Reading Desk	6. Joseph Sharp and John Spilman
12. John Wetherill, James Alcock, John Dobbs, Elizabeth Bolderham	5. Thos Cousins
13. John Westoby,Thos Brown, R Langton when there is a House on his freehold	4. Robt Ashton, Mary Kirk, Thomas Gell, Geo Epworth
14. John Wade,John Booth, Ann Langton,**Jos Dinsdale**	3. Jos Richardson, Geo Pickersgill, John Fell, Charles Berry
15. Nath'l Easton, Robt Easton, Rich'd Booth, Robert Green	2. John Barley, Elisha Wade, Willian Reed, Robt Beacock
16. Widows & single Housekeepers	1. Female servants
	Steeple

On the third day of August in the year of our Lord One Thousand Seven Hundred and Ninety-Nine at a Meeting of the Parishioners of Whitton held in their new Church the seats were appropriated to the houses by Lot, according to the plan form hereunto annexed, and the following resolutions were passed *Nemine contradicente*

1. That the churchwardens for time being shall always sit in the North East Corner of number nine.

2. If any of the farmers seats viz. No 5,6,7,9,8 10 should at any time be over filled the Overplus to have full Liberty to sit in another of the numbers which is not fill'd without asking Leave.

3. That the two Freeholders' seats viz No 12 and 13 shall mutually allow the same privilege to each other and that the five Cottagers' seats, viz No 2,3,4,14,15 shall always allow the same privilege to each other.

And lastly that any inhabitant of Mr. Goulton[12]'s. Houses in this Parish not mentioned in the plan form above shall have a Right to sit in any of the seats if not full, numbered 1,2,3,4,14,15,16,

Witness our hands on the Day and Year above written.
Wm Cookson Vicar, Rich Langton Churchwarden, Saml Butters, Thos Cousins, Thos Walker vice John his father, Joseph Sharpe, John Dobbs, John Laming, John Barley, **Joseph Dinsdale***, Thos Gell* [13]

---

[12] The Whitton LTA of 1790 showing that Thomas Goulton owned nearly all of the land in Whitton. The sums assessed actually total £13-6-2¼. (LAO: LTAs, Manley Wapentake)

[13] History of Whitton, Lincs www.diplomate.freeserve.co.uk/whitton.htm accessed July 2012 reproduced with permission. Original documents are on the Whitton parish registers (C.B. 1795-1812) 04 21 004 01A.

Joseph is one of the signatories to the document, so must have held some kind of role within the church, maybe as a warden or helper in some way (as his father before him). His gravestone had been located (below).

In Memory of Joseph Dinsdale who died 21st January 1806[14] aged 55 years
St John the Baptist's Churchyard, Whitton, Lincs.

---

[14] Whitton Parish Register records burial at 23 Jan 1806.

James Dinsdale 1785-1834[15]
Generation No. 5

JAMES[5] DINSDALE *(JOSEPH[4], JOHN[3], JOSEPH[2], THOMAS[1])* was born April 23, 1785 in Whitton, Lincs, and died 1834 in East Halton, Lincs. He married LYDIA COLLINGWOOD February 2, 1808 in Roxby cum Risby, Lincolnshire. She was born 1788, and died 1858 in East Halton, Lincs. Occupation: Farmer (on son's wedding certificate)

Children of JAMES DINSDALE and LYDIA COLLINGWOOD are:
- i. WILLIAM[6] DINSDALE, b. August 21, 1808, Roxby, Lincs; d. May 22, 1813, Roxby, Lincs.
- ii. JANE DINSDALE, b. August 4, 1811, Roxby cum Risby, Lincolnshire; d. November 23, 1830, Haltham upon Bain, Lincolnshire.
- iii. WILLIAM DINSDALE, b. April 17, 1814, Roxby cum Risby, Lincolnshire; d. 1886, Hull.
- iv. ANNE DINSDALE, b. May 11, 1816, Roxby cum Risby, Lincolnshire.
  More About ANNE DINSDALE: Source: Parish registers, Lincoln
- v. JOHN DINSDALE, b. August 3, 1819, Roxby cum Risby, Lincolnshire; d. January 1888, Yorkshire.
- vi. GEORGE DINSDALE, b. August 25, 1822, Roxby cum Risby, Lincolnshire; d. January 1862, Yorkshire.
- vii. JOSEPH DINSDALE, b. December 15, 1825, Roxby cum Risby, Lincolnshire; d. Aft. 1851.
  More About JOSEPH DINSDALE: Witness as brother Collingwood's wedding on 12 May 1851 in Keelby, Lincs
- viii. COLLINGWOOD DINSDALE, b. October 26, 1828, Roxby cum Risby, Lincs; d. July 1911, Leeds.
- ix. JANE DINSDALE, b. November 23, 1830, Haltham upon Bain, Lincs; m. JOHN DEAR.
- x. MARY DINSDALE, b. 1831.

James was born in Whitton, Lincs and, like his father, was a farmer.

Baptism Record

Baptism of James Dinsdale

on 23rd April 1785 at Whitton, Lincs

Marriage Record

Marriage of James Dinsdale to Lydia Collingwood

on 2nd February 1808 at Roxby-cum-Risby, Lincs

He married Lydia Collingwood on 2nd February 1808[16] in Roxby-cum-Risby and this is where the family settle. Lydia (1785-1858) gave birth to ten children, eight being born in Roxby then the final two girls were born in Haltham upon Bain. James Dinsdale died in 1834, and Lydia is on the 1841 census living at Hills, East Halton with some of her children.

Burial Records for James and Lydia

Burial of James Dinsdale of East Halton, Lincs

On 5th February 1834

---

[15] East Halton Parish Register, burial of James Dinsdale 5 Feb 1834, entry is next to Lydia's burial later in 1858, also in East Halton (North Killingholme Churchyard).
[16] Roxby cum Risby Parish Register, marriage on 2 Feb 1808.

Then ten years later, the census shows Lydia living at the home of her son-in-law, John Dean, born 1808 in Ferriby Sluice, Lincs, with his wife Mary and new son George Dean. Collingwood Dinsdale is also residing with this family in 1851. But, by 1858 Lydia is dead.

Right: Early Dinsdale grave found of Lydia 1785-1858

Lydia (nee Collingwood) is the mother of Collingwood Dinsdale and is buried at St Denys, North Killingholme Lincs
Lydia died 23 Feb 1858 and was buried 3 March 1858

Brother - John Dinsdale b. 1777-1815

Two Dinsdale brothers (see chart below) marry wives called Lydia and all lived in Whitton, so therefore when a Bastardy Order came to light naming "a" Lydia as having illegitimate children, it was a tangled web to sort out - especially as the illegitimate father turned out to be a third brother, Samuel; who was brother to both John and James . [17]

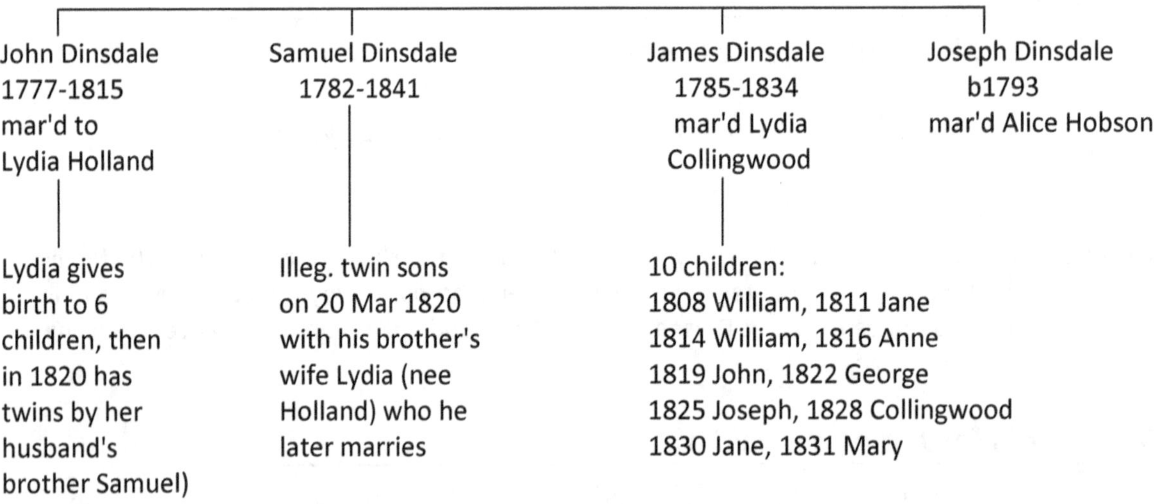

Joseph Dinsdale 1751-1806

John Dinsdale	Samuel Dinsdale	James Dinsdale	Joseph Dinsdale
1777-1815	1782-1841	1785-1834	b1793
mar'd to		mar'd Lydia	mar'd Alice Hobson
Lydia Holland		Collingwood	
Lydia gives birth to 6 children, then in 1820 has twins by her husband's brother Samuel)	Illeg. twin sons on 20 Mar 1820 with his brother's wife Lydia (nee Holland) who he later marries	10 children: 1808 William, 1811 Jane 1814 William, 1816 Anne 1819 John, 1822 George 1825 Joseph, 1828 Collingwood 1830 Jane, 1831 Mary	

---

[17] The Whitton 1831 census recorded 245 people; 134 males and 111 females in fifty-four houses. "Enclosure and agricultural improvement in North- West Lincolnshire from circa 1600 to 1850". Thomas M. Smith, MA

Generation No. 5

21. JOHN[5] DINSDALE *(JOSEPH[4], JOHN[3], JOSEPH[2], THOMAS[1])* was born March 21, 1777 in Whitton, Lincolnshire, and died August 26, 1815 in Whitton, Lincs. He married LYDIA HOLLAND January 1, 1799 in Whitton, Lincs. She was born 1779, and died June 23, 1865 in Whitton, Lincs. JOHN accidentally drowned at Whitton, age 39.

Nts: Marriage record: In the presence of Thomas Johnson and George Waddingham, John Dinsdale of the parish of Winterton, bachelor, and Lydia Holland of this Parish (Whitton) spinster were married 1st Jan 1793. Witness Joseph Dinsdale (father) and Thomas Cousins. Occupation: Waterman or labourer. Source: Whitton parish register. Lincs Marriage Index Manlake 1754-1812 Records

 Children of JOHN DINSDALE and LYDIA HOLLAND are:

  i. HANNAH[6] DINSDALE, b. December 24, 1802, Whitton, Lincs; d. March 25, 1847, Alkborough, Lincs.
  ii. MARY DINSDALE, b. May 15, 1804, Whitton, Lincs; d. 1882.
  iii. JOHN DINSDALE, b. August 22, 1805, Whitton, Lincs; d. 1846.
  iv. JOSEPH DINSDALE, b. May 24, 1807, Whitton, Lincs; d. August 3, 1807, Whitton, Lincs.
  v. JOSEPH DINSDALE, b. August 14, 1808, Whitton, Lincs; d. July 1, 1832, Barton upon Humber, Lincs.
  vi. JAMES DINSDALE, b. July 31, 1810, Whitton, Lincs; d. October 27, 1810, Whitton, Lincs.
   More About JAMES DINSDALE: Address on 1841 & 1851 census Blanket Row, Holy Trinity, Kingston upon Hull. Occupation: Mariner - 1841 census
  vii. JAMES DINSDALE, b. October 15, 1811, Whitton, Lincs; d. 1853.
  viii. WILLIAM DINSDALE, b. July 25, 1813, Whitton, Lincs; d. 1886.

22. SAMUEL[5] DINSDALE *(JOSEPH[4], JOHN[3], JOSEPH[2], THOMAS[1])* was born June 15, 1782 in Whitton, Lincolnshire, and died August 13, 1841 in Whitton, Lincolnshire. He married LYDIA HOLLAND July 16, 1822 in Kingston upon Hull, Lincolnshire. Twins he fathered by Lydia Holland, his brother's wife - see Bastardy Orders

Source: Whitton parish register

Children of SAMUEL DINSDALE and LYDIA HOLLAND are:

  i. RICHARD[6] DINSDALE, b. March 20, 1820, Whitton, Lincs; d. December 9, 1847, Glanford Brigg, Lincolnshire.
  ii. SAMUEL DINSDALE, b. March 20, 1820; d. March 17, 1851, Glanford Brigg, Lincolnshire.

Sadly John died young, aged only 39 years, cause of death being accidental drowning. He had six children with wife Lydia. Then, after his death, his wife's name is on a Bastardy Order held at Lincoln Record Office which shows that Lydia subsequently had two illegitimate children. The purpose of the Bastardy Order was to identify the father of the twins, in this case, so the father could be held to account financially for the children and they would not be a burden on the parish. So, either her family, or maybe the parish officers, ascertained from Lydia that the father of her illegitimate children was her husband's brother Samuel. Such an application was made on Lydia's behalf naming Samuel Dinsdale.[18] It should be said that Samuel does the right thing and marries Lydia some time later.

Bastardy Orders

Mother	Father	Sex	Date
Lydia Dinsdale of Whitton, twins born 20 March 1820	Samuel Dinsdale (sic) of Whitton	M	1821

The 1841 census shows Lydia (nee Holland) married to Samuel and one of their illegitimate sons Richard, aged 20 is living with them. It is thought that the following two newspaper extracts relate to two of Lydia's sons - i.e. John born 1805 (who is later recorded as a master mariner) and William born 1813:

 Whitton Packet, John Dinsdale, sails once a fortnight, four hours before high water.
 Wm Dinsdale did, in the parish of Whitton, trespass in search of game.
 One calendar month to hard labour, unless the sum of 2 l. be sooner paid.
 History, Directory and Gazetteer of the County of York, 1823.

---

[18] Lincolnshire Archives Office: LAO: WHITTON PAR/13/7 Maintenance Orders in Cases of Bastardy 1768-1828.

Tragic Death of Alice Dinsdale

Joseph Dinsdale 1793-1873 - son of Joseph - Methodist

JOSEPH[5] DINSDALE *(JOSEPH[4], JOHN[3], JOSEPH[2], THOMAS[1])* was born May 11, 1793 in Whitton, Lincolnshire, and died April 8, 1873 in Glanford Brigg, Lincoln. He married (1) ALICE HOBSON February 24, 1818 in Winterton, Lincs. She was born 1795 in Frodingham, and died 1837 in Hull. He married (2) SARAH HUNTER (NEE WESTOBY) April 23, 1840 in Whitton, Lincs. She died 1865. JOSEPH DINSDALE:Occupation: Farmer

Source: Whitton parish register - births. ALICE HOBSON: Blown up in an accident when a boiler on a steam packet she had got on exploded. Occupation: Shopkeeper

Children of JOSEPH DINSDALE and ALICE HOBSON are:

    i.   ANN[6] DINSDALE, b. December 6, 1821, Whitton, Lincolnshire; d. 1889, Glanford Brigg.

    ii.   MARY HOBSON DINSDALE, b. February 22, 1826, Whitton, Lincolnshire; m. JOSEPH COOPER, 1845.

    iii.   JOHN DINSDALE, b. February 7, 1831, Whitton, Lincolnshire.

    iv.   JOSEPH DINSDALE, b. May 10, 1833, Whitton, Lincolnshire.

         More About JOSEPH DINSDALE: Source: Whitton parish register

    v.   MARTHA DINSDALE, b. August 8, 1823, Whitton, Lincs; m. WILFRED OLDRIDGE, 1841.

Child of JOSEPH DINSDALE and SARAH WESTOBY) is:

    vi.   THOMAS WESTOBY CHESPOLEY[6] DINSDALE, b. April 6, 1841, Whitton, Lincolnshire; d. October 1895, Lancashire; m. MARIA, 1862.

It is worth mentioning Joseph Dinsdale (Jnr) born 1793 in Whitton (brother to James b. 1785 on our line of descent). Joseph (Jnr)[19] was a farmer of five acres, according to the 1851 census, but had other ideas when it came to religion. Just a few years later, on 19th June 1818, he is a signatory on an application to the Bishop of Lincoln from a group of men for a Dissenters' Certificate. They made application to make use of a house for religious worship belonging to a John Westoby for use by "His Majesty's subjects dissenting from the Church of England commonly called Independents". The other signators being: 'The Miester (sic) Mr Plumstead, John Westoby, William Smith and Edward Cambell'. *Note:* The Independents seem to have been founded by a Warrington chairmaker called Peter Phillips around 1806 and a Quaker plainness of speech and dress was apparently evident in their manner[20]. Joseph Dinsdale married in the year 1818 to Alice Hobson who was born in Frodingham in 1795, the couple marry in Winterton. Joseph was a farmer and Alice was a shopkeeper in Whitton.[21] In 1837, on Wednesday 7th June at 6 am in the morning, Alice had boarded the local Union steam packet (Hull to Gainsborough) to take a short trip from the Humber Dock Basin at Hull to Whitton[22]. Along with Alice there were about 70 other people, including crew, on the ship when tragedy struck. The boat's boiler violently exploded amongst the crowd of people sending bodies flying into the air in every direction. Alice's body was, at least, recovered but for many other relatives there were no remains to bury. Numbers of fatalities vary, according to different reports, but were anything from 20 to 100 people.[23] Alice is buried at Whitton church yard and her grave stone has the following message:-

Stop my friend and view my stone,
Consider well where I have gone.
Prepare yourselves make no delay,
For in a moment I was call'd away.

---

[19] National Probate Calendar, Probate of Wills 1858-1966. Joseph Dinsdale, 7th June "The Will of Joseph Dinsdale, late of the township of Glanford Brigg in the county of Lincoln, Yeoman, who died 8 April 1873 at Glanford Brigg was proved at Lincoln by Charles Bird of Glanford Brigg, Gentleman, the Sole Executor."

[20] History of Whitton, Lincs www.diplomate.freeserve.co.uk/whitton.htm Accessed July 2012

[21] 1842 Whitton, an extract from White's 'Gazetteer and Directory of Lincolnshire'

[22] Manchester Times, 10 June 1837

[23] Hull Advertiser 10 June 1837

COLLINGWOOD DINSDALE
1828-1911[24]

Generation No. 6

COLLINGWOOD[6] DINSDALE *(JAMES[5], JOSEPH[4], JOHN[3], JOSEPH[2], THOMAS[1])* was born October 26, 1828 in Roxby cum Risby, Lincs, and died July 1911 in Leeds. He married ANN CLARA SHEARMAN May 12, 1851 in Keelby, Lincolnshire. She was born 1830, and died 1893 in Chesterfield. On 1841 census at Thornton, Lincs age 12/13 living away from family, working as an agricultural labourer/male servant. On 1851 census living with widowed mother at Keelby, Lincs Nts: Brother Joseph is witness at his wedding & also Mary Hannah Shearman Occupation: Labourer (on marriage certificate), later agricultural labourer and cemetery keeper
More About ANN CLARA SHEARMAN: Could not write/read

Children of COLLINGWOOD DINSDALE and ANN SHEARMAN are:
   i.   ROBERT JOHN[7] DINSDALE, b. February 3, 1852, Keelby, Lincs; d. 1926, Ecclesall Bierlow, Derbyshire.
   ii. JAMES WILLIAM DINSDALE, b. June 12, 1853, Keelby, Lincs; d. 1912, Leeds.
   iii. EDWIN DINSDALE, b. September 22, 1854, Keelby, Lincs. Baptised 12 Nov 1854, source parish registers; d. January 1928, Darlington.
   iv. HENRY COLLINGWOOD DINSDALE, b. April 29, 1856, Keelby, Lincs; d. September 10, 1934, Ashton-under-Lyne.
   v.   LYDIA MARY DINSDALE, b. August 7, 1859, Keelby; d. March 15, 1860, Keelby.
   vi. SHEARMAN DINSDALE, b. May 28, 1862, Keelby, Lincs; d. August 21, 1934, Leeds.
   vii. GEORGE DINSDALE, b. February 7, 1864, Keelby, Lincs; d. 1866, Letwell, Nottinghamshire.
        More About GEORGE DINSDALE: Source: Keelby parish registers, Lincoln
   viii. FRANCES MARY DINSDALE, b. 1865, Letwell, Nottinghamshire; d. August 1937, Basford, Nottinghamshire.
   ix. CLARA DINSDALE, b. 1866; d. 1867, Letwell, Nottinghamshire.
   x.   ALFRED DINSDALE, b. 1872, Letwell, Nottingham; d. 1942, Rotherham.

Baptism Record

Collingwood was baptised on 26th October 1828 at Roxby-cum-Risby in Lincolnshire. His father James died when he was just six years of age and sadly, from the earliest census of 1841[25], we find the young 12 year old boy (so named for his mother's surname was Collingwood) working in a very small village called Thornton Curtis near Burnham in Lincolnshire living with a farming family, headed by William Story[26], as an agricultural labourer. By the next census of 1851[27], he is back living with his family in Keelby in Lincolnshire - actually with a younger sister and her husband, John Dean and his widowed mother Lydia Dinsdale is with them too.

Marriage Record

Marriage on 12th May 1851

of Collingwood Dinsdale and Ann Clara Shearman

at the Parish Church of Keelby

This must have been just weeks before Collingwood's marriage, on 12th May 1851, to Ann Clara Shearman at the Parish Church of Keelby - Ann Clara was born in that village, her father being William Shearman, a baker by profession. Sister Mary Hannah Shearman was witness at their wedding, the

---

[24]Roxby-cum-Risby parish register records baptism 26 October 1828. Free BMD Index Collingwood Dinsdale died 1911 (aged 82 Leeds 9B 480)
[25] National Archives 1841 census Collingwood Dinsdale, age 12, living with Mary Brocklesby and Thos Sinderson, both aged 20, Piece 646, book 17, folio 8, page 9.
[26] Collingwood's grandfather, Joseph (1751-1834) was married by a Robert Storry - Curate of Winteringham.
[27] National Archives 1851 census Collingwood Dinsdale, age 22, living with John Dean age 43, Mary Dean 20, George Dean age 2 and Lydia Dinsdale age 63 yrs - Appendix 1.

other witness being Joseph Dinsdale, Collingwood's older brother. The bride signs the wedding certificate, but the groom makes his mark "X". Collingwood declares his occupation to be labourer, and that of his deceased father James Dinsdale to be farmer.

Children of Collingwood Dinsdale & Ann Clara Shearman

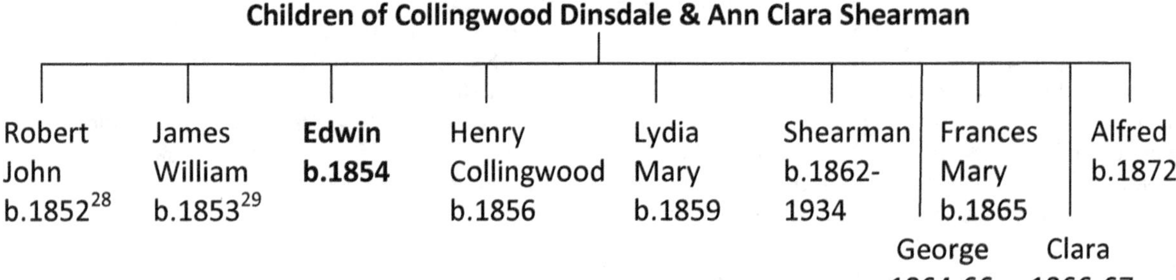

Robert John b.1852[28]	James William b.1853[29]	**Edwin b.1854**	Henry Collingwood b.1856	Lydia Mary b.1859	Shearman b.1862-1934	Frances Mary b.1865	Alfred b.1872

George 1864-66   Clara 1866-67

After marriage to Ann Clara Shearman (1831-1893), the couple settle in Keelby for some ten years and begin a family[30], their first four children all being sons. Mother Lydia dies in 1858 and the 1861 census shows Collingwood continuing to work as an agricultural labourer. But soon after this, the family relocate to Village Street in Letwell, Nottinghamshire. Their family continues to grow but the churchyard records show the burial of two infants there, George 1864-66 and Clara 1866-67.

LETWELL: St. Peter's Church, Letwell, Monumental Inscriptions. Grave number 5

In Memory of GEORGE THE BELOVED SON OF COLLINWOOD & CLARA ANN DINSDALE
WHO DIED FEBRUARY 20th 1866 AGED 2 YEARS

ALSO of CLARA THEIR DAUGHTER WHO DIED NOVEMBER 26th 1867 AGED 15 MONTHS
Mason: T. Turner, Anston

The 1871 census shows Collingwood's occupation as farm labourer still located in Letwell where more children are born, so the family's time in this place spanned some eight years or so, before another relocation. Collingwood's son Edwin, at this time, spends a couple of years in Beckingham in Nottingham but it is not known whether Collingwood's family also went there as it is a period between census returns and the birth of children so the trail to follow is not that precise. However, it is known that by1881[31]he is living at Eckington in North Derbyshire where he has achieved quite a change in employment. The 1881 census shows that he was employed as a Sexton living in a cottage next to the Church of St Peter and St Paul - the full address being Mosbro Hill Cemetery Lodge, Mill Lane, Eckington.

Cemetery Lodge, Eckington
With the church to the left

---

[28] Keelby Parish Registers, baptism of Robert John on 3 February 1852.

[29] Keelby Parish Registers, baptism of James William on 1 May 1853.

[30] National Archives 1861 Census: Collingwood Dinsdale, age 32, Ann Clara Dinsdale age 31, James Wm Dinsdale age 8, Edwin Dinsdale age 6 and Henry Collingwood Dinsdale age 4 yrs. Piece 2393, folio 71, page number 13.

[31] National Archives 1881 Census: Collingwood Dinsdale, age 57, Ann Clara Dinsdale age 50, Alfred age 9, Frances Mary age 16 and Clara Ann Dinsdale age 3. Piece 3440, folio 80, page number 3.

Collingwood's cottage is the small building in the centre which has a tiny courtyard at the rear and, across the yard, there is an outbuilding which would have been the toilet and wash house. A modest building for a growing family, but in a lovely rural setting.

A man called George Foster, who lived a few minutes away from where Collingwood Dinsdale was living in the 1880s, left a wonderful record of his Reminiscences of Mosbro[32] - dated 21st September 1886, which gives a flavour of the village life that Collingwood and his family would have experienced at that time. He describes the changes and advances that the area had seen in the 1800s, how nearly all the old thatched houses had been rebuilt into "lofty comfortable cottages", how rickety old footpaths had been asphalted and how buildings had lost their dim lighting from tallow candles as the new gas and paraffin lamps brightened them. Water was no longer carried from wells, but was piped to houses, and he was particularly pleased with the old churchyard at Eckington, where Collingwood was employed, that it was kept in order as, in earlier times, he complained that sheep were allowed to graze and "rub their greasy fleeces against the tombstones, and otherwise defile them". When Collingwood arrives in the area, the local population had doubled to 3,000 due to the nine, or more, collieries that were working - one colliery alone owned by the Wells family - employing some 500 men. Foster tells of local custom and practice and, some superstition .... for example, if a collier on his way to work caught sight of a woman, he would not go forward but would return home fearing bad luck. Sometimes the "guilty" woman would receive a "piece of his mind" for daring to be "abroad" at such an hour.

In the Eckington graveyard itself, there were claims that a woman called Ann Allen (deceased daughter of the landlord of the White Hart public house) who had been buried there, that her body was dug up and stolen by body-snatchers. Foster also recalls the practice of the local Constable who, each time he took a prisoner into his custody during the day time, took him back to his house overnight, where he chained him to his firegrate, then took him for trial the next day. Another practice, which had only just died out in the area, was called "randanning". This happened when a man had beat his wife, or committed some act of immorality (or, indeed, if a woman had done so) they were" randanned"; which meant a number of young men, followed by a crowd, would ride through the village on a cart and, at an appropriate spot near the intended target, would recite a "nominy" at the 'guilty' individuals - public humiliation if you will - which they would do for three consecutive nights and, on the last night, they would bring with them an effigy which was set fire to, as close as possible to the target's abode.

So .... this is Eckington, a place where Collingwood and his family settle for at least twenty years from at least 1881 to 1901 - possibly slightly longer - and he would have seen many of his grandchildren born and grow up there. Son Edwin also lives for a time in Eckington, though he is now married and starting his own family, so he resides at 44 Church Row, Eckington - extremely close to his father's home. Nine years later, in 1890, the son Edwin, with his family, make the move to Darlington and he is the first Dinsdale to locate there. Collingwood remains in his Cemetery Lodge with some children (and a lodger) appear on the 1891 census. However, just two years later, his wife Ann Clara dies. After her death Collingwood remains in Eckington but the 1901 census shows him living with his grand-daughter Clara Ann and her family - Clara Ann had married George Norman and they resided at 9 Littlemoor, Eckington - again close to the church area of the village.

For the rest of his days Collingwood would live with his children or grandchildren. The last census there is for him, 1911, shows him living at

Burial of Collingwood Dinsdale

August 1911, Leeds

---

[32] Reminiscences of Mosborough by George Foster, 21st September 1886.
www.oldminer.co.uk/Reminiscences%20of%20Mosborough.htm

son's family, Robert John Dinsdale. There were a total of eight Dinsdales residing in a house of just five rooms. His son was working as a joiner. He lived well into his eighties and died very shortly after the[33]1911[34] census.

Collingwood's Descendants

Son - Shearman Dinsdale 1862-1934
Shearman is shown on the census returns as working as a bricklayer, but this is his probate record: Dinsdale, Shearman of 16 Rosebank Crescent Leeds died 21 August 1934 at the General Infirmary Leeds. Administration London 5 Sept to Arthur Shearman Dinsdale, Printer.

Grandson - Arthur Dinsdale 1895-1978
Arthur is Shearman's son (b. 1895). There is, today, a Dinsdale printing company in Leeds but they claim descent from a John Dinsdale born 1801 in Leeds, wife Elizabeth, and appear not to be immediately connected.
Military Service
No full service record for Arthur, son of Shearman Dinsdale, has been found, but his name is recorded on the Memorial Notes found by Pauline Batty at Darlington Library, which state:
Dinsdale, Arthur, 70 Vancouver Street. Pte, Yorkshire Dragoons.

Daughter - Frances Mary Dinsdale 1865-1937
Daughter of Collingwood Dinsdale, Frances Mary was the first of their children to be born in Letwell, Nottingham. She marries Edwin Snape in December 1887 in Chesterfield and they have three children: Winifred Constance b.1892, Harold Edwin b. 1894 and Frances Edith b.1898. The 1891 census finds them living in Oakham, Rutland, where their first daughter Winifred Constance is born, Edwin Snape is employed as a Railway Clerk and the family live at Cow Lane, Myrtle Cottages, Oakham Deans Hold in Rutland. Ten years later, at 1901, the family has moved to Bingley in Yorkshire to 21 Manor Street and Edwin is still employed as Railway Clerk. Their remaining two children are born at Bingley. Then, another ten years forward in time, at 1911 they are at 21 Talbot Place, Sheffield where they are living in a house with 6 rooms. Frances dies in 1937 at Basford in Nottingham and, just three years later, husband Edwin dies in the same place.

Son - Henry Collingwood Dinsdale 1856-1934
Edwin Dinsdale (Senior's) brother, Henry Collingwood Dinsdale, was born 29 April 1856 in Keelby; he marries Margaret Ann Kenworthy in April 1879 at Ashton-under-Lyne and they have two daughters, also born there, Elizabeth Kenworthy Dinsdale 1881-1969 who does not appear to marry and Clara, born 1884 - dies after 1911. Although married with two daughters, on the 1891 census, he is not with them. Instead he is listed as a passenger on the ship "John Elder" (which it so happens sinks on the return journey to England some weeks/months later) travelling from London to Adelaide/Melbourne/Sidney, Australia. It is thought he spent a period of time prospecting for gold in that area before returning to the UK where he dies some years later. His departure date was 22 May 1883[35] and he is not on the UK census returns until 1901.

---

[33] National Archives 1891 Census: Collingwood Dinsdale age 64, Clara A. Age 63, Alfred age 19, Clara A, age 13, Gertrude Dinsdale, age 9 and a lodger Thomas Edgington age 74. Piece 2770, folio 24, page 42. Appendx 1.
[34] National Archives, 1911 Census: Robert John Dinsdale (joiner) head, age 59, Rebecca Dinsdale age 53, Collingwood Dinsdale age 81, Gertrude Dinsdale age 29, Robert Dinsdale age 23 (gardener), Dorothy Dinsdale age 13, Rosa Alice Dinsdale age 10 and Margaret Dinsdale age 6.
[35] Unassisted Passenger Lists to Australia, 1883. The John Elder was an 1870 built passenger cargo ship.

EDWIN DINSDALE (Senior)

1854-1928

Generation No. 7

EDWIN[7] DINSDALE (*COLLINGWOOD[6], JAMES[5], JOSEPH[4], JOHN[3], JOSEPH[2], THOMAS[1]*) was born September 22, 1854 in Keelby, Lincs. Baptised 12 Nov 1854, source parish registers, and died January 1928 in Darlington. He married ELLEN/ELEANOR GURNHILL July 30, 1877 in Christchurch, Attercliffe, Sheffield. She was born 1854 in Beckingham, Notts/Lincs Border, and died January 1928 in Darlington.

More About EDWIN DINSDALE: On 1911 census at 8 Minor Street, Darlington. Died of cerebral thrombosis. Grandson A. O'Connor present at death. Owned own house in Stapleton, built a bungalow in his garden for son Arnold. House left to Anthony O'Connor, grandson. Living at 19 Alliance Street, Darlington at marriage. Nts: Edwin was lodging on the 1901 census at 1522 Walker Road, Newcastle on Tyne. Family were living at 1 Foundry Street, Darlington on 1901 census. Occupation: Forge Labourer, gasworks stoker, gardener, works watchman

Children of EDWIN DINSDALE and ELLEN/ELEANOR GURNHILL are:
 i. ELEANOR[8] DINSDALE, b. May 5, 1878, Beckingham, Notts/Lincs Border; d. 1957, Durham.
 ii. CLARA ANN DINSDALE, b. July 4, 1881, Beckingham, Nottinghamshire; d. December 1952, Darlington.
 iii. FRED DINSDALE, b. November 13, 1882, Eckington, Derbyshire; d. February 5, 1955, Friargate Hospital, Richmond, North Yorkshire; m. HILDA MARY WALTON, August 1941, Richmond, North Yorkshire; b. March 28, 1894, Thirsk, Yorkshire; d. October 22, 1975, Darlington.
 More About FRED DINSDALE: Probate: to widow Hilda Mary granted 26th March, effects £1319 12s 7d. Occupation: Grocer on 1911 census and 1928 Admon for his Father Edwin - he was the eldest son and was granted Administration of his father's estate.
 iv. ARNOLD DINSDALE, b. 1887, Eckington, Derbyshire; d. May 21, 1953, Darlington.
 v. LYDIA DINSDALE, b. August 31, 1888, Eckington, Derbyshire; d. March 1971, Darlington.
 vi. JOHN COLLINGWOOD DINSDALE, b. 1890, Darlington; d. April 12, 1891, Darlington.
 vii. WALTER COLLINGWOOD DINSDALE, b. 1893, Darlington; d. April 26, 1915, Ypres, Menin Gate, Belgium.
 More About WALTER COLLINGWOOD DINSDALE:
 Nts: Died in the 1st World War, served in France, medals: Victory, British and Star Medals
 viii. EDWIN DINSDALE, b. September 1, 1896, Holy Trinity Church, Darlington; d. May 20, 1946, Darlington.

To distinguish Edwin Dinsdale, born 1896, the central figure in this research, from his father of the same name, born 1854, we refer to them as 'Junior' and 'Senior'.

Birth Record

<table><tr><td>Birth in 1854 in Keelby

of Collingwood Dinsdale</td></tr></table>

Edwin Dinsdale (Senior) son of Collingwood Dinsdale, was born in 1854 in Keelby, Lincs but he wasn't to stay in Lincolnshire for long because, by the age of 10 years, his father relocated the family to Letwell in the area of South Yorkshire/North Nottinghamshire where father Collingwood was engaged as a farm worker. Edwin had only a few years to live in Letwell before he was sent away from home to work in service to a Charles Joseph Muddiman, a Northampton shoe manufacturer and his family, who were living at 110 Upper Hanover Street in Sheffield which would have been about 15 miles away from his parents' home. Edwin is just 16 years of age (though the census records of 1871 state age 15) and employed as a groom to the family. The family business appears in trade directories as having premises at 20 Angel Street and 1 King Street in Sheffield.[36]

---

[36] 1893 Kelly's Director of Leeds, Sheffield and Rotherham.

On the 1871 census, whilst Edwin is working as a groom in Sheffield, Ellen/Eleanor is in general service, some 36 miles away, to John and Jane Leggott who were licensed victuallers of the Crooked Billet, Owston Ferry, in west Lincolnshire. At some time in the early 1870s Edwin leaves his job as a groom to begin working as a coal miner.

Eckington Collieries

During the 1880s, when Edwin was employed there, Eckington was a huge site comprising of ten or more collieries. The tiny rural village population swelled to 3,000 as the mine proprietors - the Wells family - needed more and more men and boys to extract the coal.

Working conditions were dreadful, with reports of underground flooding, collapses and explosions. But the demand for coal was high and the mine owners paid 10 shillings for an eight hour day (50p). Discipline was harsh.
In 1888, two young boys were jailed for seven days for stealing three stones of coal.

Edwin's address on the census was 44 Church Row in Eckington - which may have been either rented or tied accommodation probably owned by the mine.

It is known that the Dinsdales stayed in Eckington throughout the 1880s but, by the next census in 1891, Edwin was in Darlington and employed as a Labourer at the Gasworks.

1911 finds Edwin working at the Forge Works at Darlington.

URDAY, APRIL 9, 1881.

SHOCKING FATALITIES AT ECKINGTON.

On Saturday, Mr. Busby, jun., coroner, held an enquiry at the Royal Hotel, Eckington, touching the death of George Elliott, collier, of Eckington, who died on the 31st March at Eckington. The facts of the case were very simple, and were as follows :— Deceased, who was 18 years of age, went to his work in the Renishaw Park Colliery, in a stall along with several other men, the place being considered in a safe and workable condition. Work had been carried on some time when deceased had occasion to lean over the top of one of the "corves," and, while doing so a fall of rock occurred. The result was that deceased's body being between the tub and the rock, he was crushed most fearfully, from which injuries he died in a short time. Several witnesses were called, and all agreed that no blame could by any possibility be attached to anyone, and the jury returned a verdict that death was accidental, with which finding the Coroner quite concurred.

Another inquest was held at the Royal Hotel, on Monday, by Mr. S. G. N. Spofforth, deputy coroner, on the body of a child named Louisa Little, aged 15 months, whose shocking death was to a certain extent the outcome of the previous case. Deceased was the daughter of a collier named Henry Little, who resided at Eckington. It transpired that the child's mother was one of the persons who was preparing for the interment of the young man Elliott (particulars of whose death is given above) and deceased was left in the care of a sister aged about ten years. The mother was sent for, it being stated that the child had fallen from a table, and on going home she found that the child had apparently had a heavy fall, and alighted on her head on the floor. She was bruised and shaken, and the girl in charge accounted for the injuries by saying that deceased had fallen from a table on to her head. Dr. Jones was sent for, but deceased did not rally. After a short consultation, a verdict of "Accidental Death", was given in this as in the above case.

The South Yorkshire coalfields were centred around the Sheffield area where he had been in service, and he next surfaces in Attercliffe in 1877 - when he marries Ellen/Eleanor Gurnhill[37].

Marriage Record

Marriage in Attercliffe in 1877

of Edwin Dinsdale to Ellen Gurnhill

Ellen was born in Beckingham to Hezekiah Gurnhill and Elizabeth Harwood who both came from Upton in Lincolnshire. Curiously Hezekiah is referred to on the 1861 census as being a "huckster" which, depending which definition you wish to believe, made him a "pedlar of shoddy goods"! So Beckingham is where Edwin and Ellen/Eleanor's first two children are born. Both Attercliffe and Beckingham had large coal collieries and, no doubt, Edwin's employment brought him into that area - unless they were living near to her family. The 1881 census shows Edwin living with his growing family, now in Eckington - which again was an area totally dominated by mining activities and the census shows he was, indeed, working as a coal miner there.

CHRONOLOGY

1854	Keelby, Lincs	(Born)
1864	Letwell, Notts	(Scholar)
1871	Sheffield	(Working in service as a Groom)
1877	Attercliffe	(Marries)
1878-80	Beckingham	(Birth of youngest children)
1881-88	Eckington	(Census & birth of children)

1890 - Edwin moves to Darlington

Edwin Senior had relocated his family from the South Yorkshire coalfields area to Darlington where he initially works as a labourer in the gas works before taking up a post at the Darlington Forge Company - one of the largest local employers - which incidentally is where many of his children will later work.

LOCATIONS WITHIN DARLINGTON

EDWIN SENIOR'S FAMILY:-

YEAR	ADDRESS	SOURCES
1890-96	19 Alliance Street	Birth of sons John Collingwood, Walter and Edwin (Jnr)
1901*	1 Foundry Street, Harrogate Hill	1901 Census - Appendix 2
1911-12	8 Minor Street	1911 Census - Appendix 2
1913-28	The Green, Stapleton, Croft	Edwin dies at this address
*1901	St Anthony, Byker, Newcastle	Edwin boarding/working away from home at 1901 census

---

[37] Marriage Certificate of Edwin Dinsdale (Snr) 1877, 30th July and Eleanor (Helen) Dinsdale, states both same age at marriage i.e. 23 years. His father Collingwood Dinsdale - labourer, place at time of marriage Attercliffe. Her father was John Gurnhill, farmer. Witnesses at wedding John Matthews and Marilyn Jane Gurnhill.

Edwin Arrives in Darlington aged 36 yrs

Edwin Senior's initial residence in Darlington shows the family living at Alliance Street. Then, with each subsequent census record, there are further changes of address as follows:

1890-96	19 Alliance Street, Darlington	(Birth of sons John, Walter & Edwin)
1901	1 Foundry Street, Darlington	(Family here on 1901 census)
1911-12	8 Minor Street, Darlington	(1911 census & son's attestation)
1913-28	The Green, Stapleton, Darlington	(address on death certificate)

Edwin's last house move, just before the outbreak of the First World War, was to be his last as he remains living at The Green in Stapleton until his death.   Most of Edwin's sons do not appear to have moved with their parents to Stapleton - with the exception of Arnold. By 1913, the children were all grown up and, even the youngest Edwin Jnr, was in full time employment at the Darlington Forge Company. The War Memorial documentation[38] shows that by 1913 to 1914, son Fred was living at 10 Willow Road, Darlington and younger brothers Walter and Edwin were right next door to Fred at number 8 Willow - probably all were in lodgings.

Pictured below - Edwin Dinsdale's house on The Green at Stapleton, near Darlington.

Picture courtesy of Pauline Batty and Peter Dinsdale (Arnold's grandson)

Edwin Dinsdale (Senior) dies on 10th February 1928 at Stapleton Croft at this house. His primary cause of death was a cerebral thrombosis and his death certificate states that there was no post-mortem. Present at the time of his death was his grandson, Anthony O'Connor and the death was registered on 11th February, the day following his death.

---

[38] War Memorial Documentation, list held by Darlington Library, showing list of men who fought in World War I and their addresses at time of enlistment.

Edwin's house was in the family's possession for almost 70 years:

1913   Moves into above house at The Green, Stapleton
1928   Dies at the house
1928   Wife dies the same year
1928   Grandson Anthony O'Connor (age 27 and newly married) lives there
1956   Anthony's wife Sarah (Sally) dies
1958   Anthony remarries to Irene (a Dinsdale cousin)
1976   Anthony's death. His Will allows wife Irene to live her life out there.
1981   Wife Irene dies
1981   Anthony's Will, house passes to god-daughter Sally Caseley
1981   Sally sells the house to unknown purchaser.

The High Court records state[39]:

"BE IT KNOWN that Edwin Dinsdale of Stapleton in the County of York died on the 10th day of February 1928 at Stapleton aforesaid intestate, a widower. AND BE IT FURTHER KNOWN that, at the date hereunder written, Letters of Administration of all the Estate which by law devolves to and vests in the personal representative of the said intestate were granted by His Majesty's High Court of Justice at the District Probate Registry thereof at York to Fred Dinsdale of 1 Reeth Road, Richmond, in the said County, Grocer, the lawful son and one of the persons entitled to share in the estate
Of which the said intestate dated the 9th Day of January 1928. Gross value of estate £130:11:8
Extracted by the Administrator. Sureties: James Henry Woodward of West Field Richmond, retired farmer and George Robinson of 1 Cornforth Hill, Richmond, grocer proprietor."
Note: The date at the bottom of the document must be in error, and should have read "dated the 9th day of January 1929".

So, Edwin's eldest son Fred handled the administration of the estate. It is also interesting to note that Edwin is referred to as a widower. The records show both he and his wife Ellen/Eleanor die in the same first quarter of 1928 but, clearly, his wife died first and Edwin within a few weeks of her. Both die intestate. The bungalow which was built in Edwin's garden, see picture below, was for his son Arnold.

Picture courtesy of Pauline Batty and Peter Dinsdale (Arnold's grandson)
It is thought that the bungalow was built not long after Edwin's arrival in Stapleton in 1913 - the same year that Arnold married. Edwin Senior's house would have been too small to accommodate any of his

---

[39] Admon Probate Records.

sons and building the bungalow would have allowed Arnold to live nearby. It is known that Arnold raised his family at the bungalow and was still there in 1939. He was employed as a plumber. But, by 1947, his first wife Margaret Lewins has died and this seems to coincide with him leaving the bungalow. Within a year he has remarried to the, now widowed, Edith Dinsdale (nee Middleton) and he goes to live at Edith's home.   The bungalow must have continued in the family, after Arnold's departure, as his grandson Peter (son of Eric) and wife Barbara - who married in 1964 - recall being in the bungalow quite well, so it must have remained connected with the family for at least 40 years. Edwin was buried at St Peter's, Croft Cemetery, but there is no headstone for either Edwin or wife Eleanor.[40]

CHILDREN OF EDWIN AND ELEANOR DINSDALE

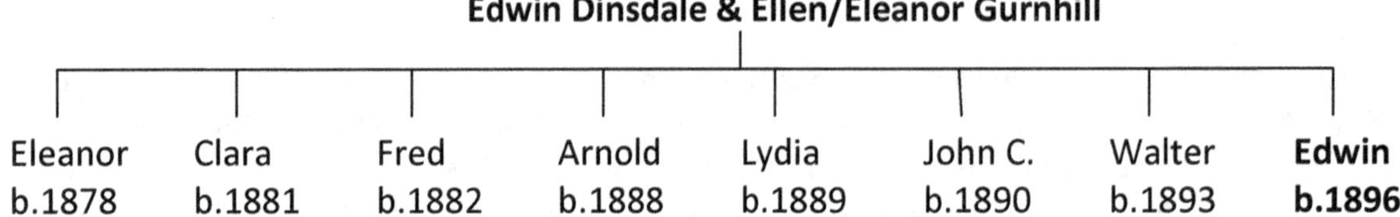

Generation No. 8

Eldest daughter Eleanor

ELEANOR[8] DINSDALE (*EDWIN[7], COLLINGWOOD[6], JAMES[5], JOSEPH[4], JOHN[3], JOSEPH[2], THOMAS[1]*) was born May 5, 1878 in Beckingham, Notts/Lincs Border, and died 1957 in Durham. She married JOHN JOSEPH O'CONNOR January 26, 1901 in Stanley Chapel, Lanchester, Durham. He was born 1859 in Ireland, and died April 1904 in Darlington. More About JOHN JOSEPH O'CONNOR: Married twice: two sons from 1st marriage: John and Arthur

Children of ELEANOR DINSDALE and JOHN O'CONNOR are:

    i. ANTHONY[9] O'CONNOR, b. February 25, 1901, Durham; d. October 28, 1976, Darlington; m. (1) SARAH DONALDSON, June 14, 1926, Croft, near Darlington; b. 1897, Darlington; d. 1956, Darlington; m. (2) IRENE MARY CORNFORTH, 1958, Darlington; b. 1921, Middlesbrough; d. December 1981, Darlington.
      More About ANTHONY O'CONNOR:On 1911 census living with grandparents
      Nts: Witness at wedding of Edwin (1896-1946) and Edith Middleton
      Present at death of Edwin Dinsdale Snr (1854-1928)
      More About SARAH DONALDSON:
      Notes On 1911 census at 15 Green Street Darlington living with widowed mother & brother Joseph b 1896.
      Nts: At Anthony O'Connor's death, Joseph's son John William 1920-2003 is bequeathed land at Cleasby Road, Stapleton, nr Darlington
    ii. EDWIN O'CONNOR, b. 1903, Langley Moor, Durham; d. 1970, Darlington.

Generation No. 8

Second daughter Clara

CLARA ANN[8] DINSDALE (*EDWIN[7], COLLINGWOOD[6], JAMES[5], JOSEPH[4], JOHN[3], JOSEPH[2], THOMAS[1]*) was born July 4, 1881 in Beckingham, Nottinghamshire, and died December 1952 in Darlington. She married FREDERICK SYDNEY GRIEVESON December 27, 1903 in Darlington. He was born 1882 in Darlington, and died 1925 in Darlington.Notes: Emigrates with family for 10 years to Ohio, Lagrange, Lorraine, in America 1909-1919 approx. FREDERICK SYDNEY GRIEVESON: Trackman working on Ohio Railway, in America 1909-1919 approx.

Child of CLARA DINSDALE and FREDERICK GRIEVESON is:

    i. EDWIN COLLINGWOOD GODLEY[9] GRIEVESON, b. September 16, 1908; d. March 1984, Darlington; m. ALICE MIRIAM M CLEMINSON, December 1950, Darlington; b. June 1906, South Shields; d. January 1993, Darlington. More About EDWIN COLLINGWOOD GODLEY GRIEVESON: Joint Executor of Antony O'Connor's Will in 1976 at which time Edwin's address was 15 Dundee Street Darlington.

---

[40] Monumental Inscriptions, Croft and Hurworth. Cleveland Family History Society.

Generation No. 8

Eldest son Fred

See previous section 'Siblings of Edwin Dinsdale Jnr'.

Generation No. 8

Second son Arnold

Also, see previous section 'Siblings of Edwin Dinsdale Jnr'.

ARNOLD[8] DINSDALE (*EDWIN[7], COLLINGWOOD[6], JAMES[5], JOSEPH[4], JOHN[3], JOSEPH[2], THOMAS[1]*) was born 1887 in Eckington, Derbyshire, and died May 21, 1953 in Darlington. He married (1) MARGARET A. LEWINS 1913 in Darlington. She was born 1888 in York, and died 1947 in North Allerton. He married (2) EDITH ANN MIDDLETON July 1948 in Darlington. She was born September 24, 1899 in Cotherstone, Yorkshire, and died May 17, 1972 in Darlington. Arnold had a prosthetic hand by 1948, but not at 1939 when he was working as a plumber.

More About EDITH ANN MIDDLETON: Edith's 3rd marriage to Harry Dunn was not valid as he already had a living wife. Edith married 2ndly to Edwin's brother Arnold. Address at marriage 24 Wycombe Street, Darlington Nts: Buried West Cemetery, Darlington

Children of ARNOLD DINSDALE and MARGARET LEWINS are:
    i.   ERIC[9] DINSDALE, b. May 19, 1914, Darlington; d. March 28, 2007.
   ii.   IRENE MARY DINSDALE, b. 1916, Darlington; d. 1981.
  iii.   WALTER COLLINGWOOD DINSDALE, b. 1919, Darlington; d. 1991, Cleveland.

Generation No. 8

Third daughter, Lydia

LYDIA[8] DINSDALE (*EDWIN[7], COLLINGWOOD[6], JAMES[5], JOSEPH[4], JOHN[3], JOSEPH[2], THOMAS[1]*) was born August 31, 1888 in Eckington, Derbyshire, and died March 1971 in Darlington. She married ARTHUR CHILTON November 1912 in Darlington. He was born 1887 in Darlington, and died 1957 in Darlington.

Child of LYDIA DINSDALE and ARTHUR CHILTON is:
    i.   ARTHUR[9] CHILTON, b. 1913, Darlington; d. 1913, Darlington.

Generation No. 8

Fifth son Edwin (Junior)

See next section of book.

Move to Stapleton

As already mentioned, in 1913, just before the start of the First World War, Edwin (Snr) moves to Stapleton with his wife and grandchildren. Stapleton was a small village of 940 acres, but over 220 acres of land in the village had been bought up by the Duke of Cleveland (Lord Darlington) for charity purposes. He used the land to build almshouses. Edwin Senior's great-grandson, via son Arnold/Eric, Peter Staley Dinsdale (b. 1940) tells that Edwin, in fact, owned his own home and, at his death in 1928, the house passed to grandson Anthony O'Connor (grocer). Anthony was only 3 years old when his father, John Joseph O'Connor (who had married Eleanor - Edwin Senior's eldest daughter), had died in 1904 and the 1911 census shows him living with his grandparents, who no doubt helped raise him, along with his mother Eleanor (nee Dinsdale). Anthony O'Connor's Will (see page 39). When Anthony O'Connor dies in 1974, his wife Irene, who dies later in 1981, lived there for the rest of her days. At her death, the property was sold.

Peter also believed that Edwin (snr) had a bungalow built in the grounds of the garden for son Arnold to live in.

Death Record

Death Certificate for Edwin Dinsdale,

aged 73 years

Died 10th February 1928, Stapleton Croft

Pictured right:- Eric 1914-2007 (son of Arnold Dinsdale) married Betty Hodgson (1915-2008) in 1939 in Darlington.

They had two children - a daughter Mary, who sadly lived less than a year and a son Peter. Peter marries Barbara Edwards in 1964 in Darlington.
Peter and Barbara have two children: Helen Jane, born 1965 and Rachel Ann born 1967 - all in Darlington

Peter and partner Lynne recalled the houses that Arnold and his father Edwin (senior) lived in at their time in Stapleton. Arnold lived in a bungalow built in Edwin's garden and the rooms were very large.

Generation No. 9

ERIC[9] DINSDALE (*ARNOLD[8], EDWIN[7], COLLINGWOOD[6], JAMES[5], JOSEPH[4], JOHN[3], JOSEPH[2], THOMAS[1]*) was born May 19, 1914 in Darlington, and died March 28, 2007. He married BETTY HODGSON August 5, 1939 in Darlington. She was born August 24, 1915, and died August 8, 2008. Eric was the informant at the death of Irene M O'Connor (nee Dinsdale) - sister

Children of ERIC DINSDALE and BETTY HODGSON are:
- i. PETER STALEY[10] DINSDALE, b. July 12, 1940.
- ii. MARY DINSDALE, b. August 14, 1948, Darlington; d. January 1949, Darlington.

Arnold's son Eric lived in Richmond, Yorkshire and, as a teenager, worked in a shop for his Uncle Fred Dinsdale.

The O'Connors

Represented below, a diagram, showing the O'Connors' central role in the Dinsdale family

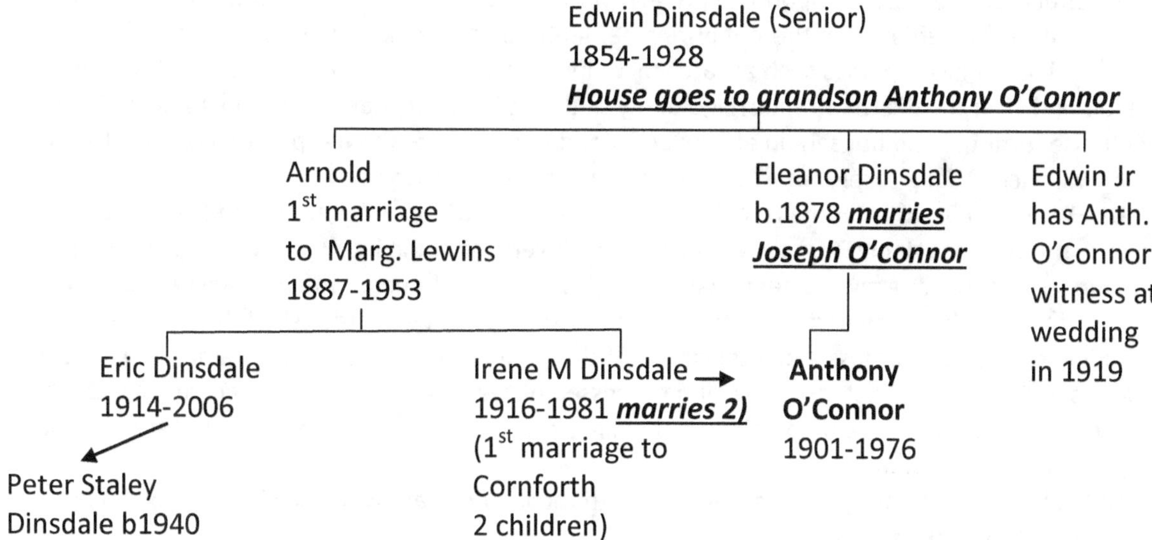

Anthony O'Connor seems to connect to several members of the Dinsdale family over some forty years. He is witness at Edwin Dinsdale (Jnr) and Edith Middleton's marriage in 1919, then later marries their niece Irene Dinsdale.... Irene's first marriage was to Lawrence Cornforth and they lived at 2 Cleveland Terrace in Darlington - though she doesn't marry O'Connor until 1958, long, long after Edwin Senior's demise. Edwin Senior did not leave a Will.

Probate of Anthony O'Connor

In the High Court of Justice, The District Probate Registry at Newcastle Upon Tyne
BE IT KNOWN that ANTHONY O'CONNOR of The Green Stapleton Darlington County Durham died on the 28th Day of October 1976. Administration to EDWIN COLLINGWOOD GODLEY GRIEVESON (in the Will called Edwin Grieveson) of 15 Dundee Street Darlington aforesaid and FRANCIS JACOB GRAY (in the Will called Frank Gray) of 65 Longfield Road Darlington aforesaid the Executors named in the said Will. Estate value £12,735.03, net £12,535.13, dated 6th day of January 1977. *Clayhills Lucas & Co., 84 Grange Road, Darlington, County Durham DL1 5NR Solicitors*

Will of Anthony O'Connor

This is the last Will and Testament of me ANTHONY O'CONNOR of The Green Stapleton in the North Riding of Yorkshire. Retired Grocer.
I HEREBY REVOKE all former Wills and testamentary dispositions heretofore made by me and declare this to be my last Will.
I APPOINT Edwin Grieveson of 15 Dundee Street Darlington in the County of Durham and Frank Gray of 54 Longfield Road Darlington aforesaid (hereinafter called "my Trustees") to be the Executors and Trustees of this my Will.
1. I GIVE to each of my Trustees if they shall prove my Will the sum of ten pounds.
2. I GIVE the money due to me from the Navy Army and Air Force Institutes Superannuation Fund to my wife Irene Mary O'Connor absolutely.

3. I GIVE to my nephew John William Donaldson the son of Joseph Donaldson the monies in my account at the Yorkshire Bank Limited Darlington

4. I DEVISE my garden land situate off the Cleasby Road at Stapleton to my Trustees Upon Trust to sell the same with power to postpone the sale thereof and to hold Upon Trust the net proceeds thereof for my said Nephew John William Donaldson.

5. I DEVISE my dwellinghouse situated at The Green Stapleton aforesaid together with my furniture and household effects to my Trustees Upon Trust to allow my wife Irene Mary O'Connor if she shall survive me to have the use and enjoyment thereof during her lifetime or so long as she remains my widow she being responsible for all outgoings such as rates taxes insurance and for the keeping of the house in good repair and after the death or remarriage of my said wife I DIRECT that my Trustees shall sell my dwellinghouse furniture and household effects and stand possessed of the net proceeds of sale Upon Trust for my Godchild Sally Caseley of 47 Mylodon Road Lowestoft absolutely.

6. I GIVE DEVISE AND BEQUEATH the remainder of my estate of whatsoever nature and wheresoever situate unto my Trustees Upon Trust to sell call in and convert the same into money at such time or times and in such manner as my Trustees shall think fit with power to postpone the sale calling in or conversion of the whole or any part or parts thereof for so long as my Trustees shall think proper without being responsible for loss and after payment thereout of my funeral and testamentary expenses death duties and debts my Trustees shall stand possessed of the residue of the said monies or of such part of my Estate as shall for the time being remain unsold and unconverted Upon Trust for my said wife Irene Mary O'Connor absolutely.

7. I DESIRE to be cremated and my ashes interred with those of my late wife Sally in the grave of our grandparents in Croft Parish Churchyard.

IN WITNESS whereof I the said Anthony O'Connor have hereunto set my hand to this my last Will this twenty-fifth day of July One thousand nine hundred and sixty-six.

SIGNED by the above Testator as and for his last Will in the presence of us both being present at the same time who at his request and in his presence and in the presence of each other we have hereunto subscribed our names as witnesses: T G Robinson and Ian T Todd, Clerks with Clayhills Lucas Solicitors. Darlington.

Explanation

Anthony marries twice; firstly to Sarah Donaldson and secondly to Irene Mary Cornforth (nee Dinsdale, his cousin, both being grandchildren of Edwin Dinsdale Senior), he has no children from either marriage. He names Edwin Grieveson as Joint Executor. Grieveson is the son of Clara Ann Dinsdale (Anthony's Aunt). His house at The Green Stapleton, which he assumed after the demise of Edwin Dinsdale Senior, is bequeathed to a god-daughter (after his wife's death), the god-daughter being Sally R. Caseley (b. 1952 in Lothingland Suffolk and marries in 1971 to Robert Coates).

Then, he bequeaths a separate parcel of land he owns off Cleasby Road at Stapleton to his "nephew" John William Donaldson - actually a nephew of his first wife Sarah Donaldson. First wife Sarah must also have gone by the name Sally as he requests his ashes to be buried with hers at Croft Cemetery in Darlington. The following picture shows a house built by Donaldson, on the land between Edwin Senior's house and that of his son Arnold Dinsdale.

EDWIN DINSDALE (Junior)
1896-1946

Generation 8

EDWIN[8] DINSDALE (*EDWIN[7], COLLINGWOOD[6], JAMES[5], JOSEPH[4], JOHN[3], JOSEPH[2], THOMAS[1]*) was baptised September 1, 1896 in Holy Trinity Church, Darlington, and died May 20, 1946 in Darlington. He married EDITH ANN MIDDLETON April 21, 1919 in Holy Trinity Church, Darlington. She was born September 24, 1899 in Cotherstone, Yorkshire, and died May 17, 1972 in Darlington. Edwin's Address at marriage 15 Newfoundland Street, Darlington Buried West Cemetery, Darlington Occupation: Pattern-maker. Edith's address at marriage 24 Wycombe Street, Darlington. Edith married secondly to Edwin's brother Arnold; Edith's third marriage to Harry Dunn was not valid as he already had a living wife. Edith is buried West Cemetery, Darlington

Children of EDWIN DINSDALE and EDITH MIDDLETON are:
  i.   ELSIE[9] DINSDALE, b. October 6, 1919, Darlington; d. December 1984, Darlington.
  ii. LAURA DINSDALE, b. February 11, 1921, Darlington; d. January 23, 1997, Derby.
  iii. MARJORIE ELEANOR DINSDALE, b. July 23, 1923, Darlington; d. June 1988, Darlington.
  iv. MAURICE EDWIN DINSDALE, b. July 23, 1923, Darlington; d. February 1993, Darlington.
  v.   JOYCE DINSDALE, b. July 15, 1928, Darlington; d. June 1972, Darlington.
  vi. MAUREEN DINSDALE, b. February 1931, Darlington; d. November 2002, Darlington.

As already mentioned, Edwin Senior brings his family to Darlington in 1890; son John being the first to be born there, then Walter in 1893 and, lastly, Edwin Junior in 1896.

Birth Record

Birth Certificate for Edwin Dinsdale (Jnr) 1896-1946 - born 1st September 1896 in Darlington.

LOCATIONS WITHIN DARLINGTON

EDWIN SENIOR'S FAMILY:-

YEAR	ADDRESS	SOURCES
1890-96	19 Alliance Street	Birth of sons John Collingwood, Walter and Edwin (Jnr)
1901*	1 Foundry Street, Harrogate Hill	1901 Census - Appendix 2
1911-12	8 Minor Street	1911 Census - Appendix 2
1913-28	The Green, Stapleton, Croft	Edwin dies at this address
*1901	St Anthony, Byker, Newcastle	Edwin boarding/working away from home at 1901 census

EDWIN JUNIOR'S FAMILY:-

YEAR	ADDRESS	SOURCES
1914	8 Willow Road*	Lodging with brother Walter
1919	15 Newfoundland Street	Marriage Certificate -
1920-24	24 Wycombe Street	Wife's Middleton family home**
1925-27	25 Valley Street	Electoral Rolls
1928-29	41 Archer Street	Electoral Rolls & daughter Joyce's birth
1930-33	25 Valley Street	Electoral Rolls & daughter Maureen's birth
1934-52	16 Hundens Lane East	Edwin died at this address.
1952-72	34 Kirkstall Crescent	Edwin's widowed wife, Edith Annie lived here, with daughter Elsie next door at number 27.

*   1914   10 Willow Road, Darlington   Lodging next door brother Fred Dinsdale
** 1921   24 Wycombe Street, Darlington   Marriages from here of daughters Laura & Marjorie

Edith Annie Dinsdale (nee Middleton)

1919-24	24 Wycombe Street*, Darlington	(Marriage Cert/parents' home)
1925	25 Valley Street**, Darlington	(Electoral Roll)
1928-29	41 Archer Street, Darlington	(Birth cert of Joyce & Electoral Roll)
1930-33	25 Valley Street, Darlington	(Birth cert of Maureen & Electoral Roll)
1934-52	16 Hundens Lane East, Darlington	Dau Laura marries from here in 1942 & 1948
1952-72[41]	34 Kirkstall Crescent, Darlington	Dau Elsie lives next door (no. 27)

Miscellaneous

*1941	24 Wycombe Street, Darlington	(Marjorie Eleanor's address at marriage)
* 1952	16 Valley Street, Darlington	(Addr. of Joyce's husband at marriage)

CHRONOLOGY - Edwin Dinsdale (Jnr)

1896	**Birth**
1910-12	LEFT ALBERT ROAD SCHOOL, AGED 14 OR 15 YRS, TO WORK FOR THE FORGE COMPANY
1911	ERRAND BOY - MILK (ON 1911 CENSUS)
1912	WORKING AS A PATTERNMAKER FOR THE DARLINGTON FORGE COMPANY
1912-13	SIGNS UP FOR MILITARY SERVICE (AGED 17 YRS 2 MONTHS), DURHAM LIGHT INFANTRY
1914	HIS BATTALION WAS STATIONED AT WEST HARTLEPOOL
1915	CONTINUES MILITARY SERVICE – SENT TO FRANCE XMAS 1915 (AGE 19)
1916	EXPEDITIONARY FORCE IN FRANCE 27.5.16 TO 1918
1917	20TH DECEMBER. APPOINTED LANCE CORPORAL INITIALLY UNPAID.
1918	AWARDED MILITARY MEDAL – 17 APRIL 1918
1918	AWARDED WAR MEDAL

---

[41] Edith was among the first tenants on the newly built Council Housing Estate, 'Bransome' in Cockerton.
1953: Revised plans submitted for erection of 204 dwellings on Branksome Drive Estate - Electrical Times: Volume 123

1918	AWARDED VICTORY MEDAL
1918	DISCHARGED FROM SERVICE – INJURED RIGHT SHOULDER. ISSUED WITH THE WAR BADGE
1919	MARRIES (AGE 25) EDITH MIDDLETON AND INITIALLY LIVES WITH HER FAMILY
1919	BIRTH OF FIRST DAUGHTER, ELSIE
1921	BIRTH OF SECOND DAUGHTER, LAURA
1923	BIRTH OF TWINS, FIRST SON MAURICE AND THIRD DAUGHTER MARJORIE
1928	BIRTH OF FOURTH DAUGHTER, JOYCE
1928	DEATH OF HIS FATHER
1931	BIRTH OF FIFTH DAUGHTER, MAUREEN
1940s	EDWIN WORKS AS COMMISSIONAIRE AT THE DARLINGTON FORGE COMPANY
1946	EDWIN DIES (OF LUNG CANCER) 20TH MAY 1946

ALBERT ROAD SCHOOL

Edwin attended Albert Road School in Darlington, along with his brothers Arnold and Walter. The school was demolished many years ago, but there does remain an oak Memorial Plaque for the 1914-18 First World War period listing all the school's pupils who served their country, which lists all three brothers[42].

The plaque was once to be found in Darlington Museum but, since that has now closed, it has been relocated to the basement of Darlington Library.

DARLINGTON FORGE COMPANY

Edwin (and his father before him[43]) worked for the Darlington Forge Company which was the second biggest employer in Darlington at the time ....

The company had a long history in the area, dating back to 1854. Edwin's attestation papers show, when he signed up for military service in 1912, that he was already employed by the company as a patternmaker. So it would seem that he stayed with the same employer for his whole life, as his death certificate shows him working as a commissioner for the forge company.

Three generations of Dinsdales would work for this company:-

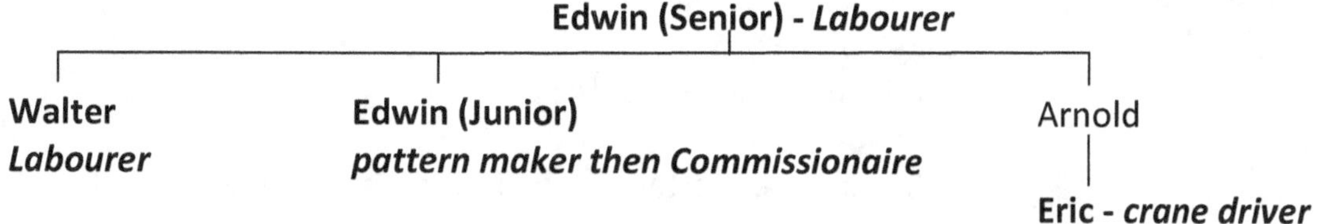

---

[42] Announced in the Northern Echo on 21 Feb 1920, page 5, column 2.

[43] Death certificate for Edwin Dinsdale Senior, refers to him as "formerly a forge labourer"

MILITARY SERVICE

Information from War Records

1912	Joined TA on 23 February 1912[44]
1912	Attestation/Signing Up Papers for 4 Years Territorial Force (age 17 years 2 months) Army no. 1436
	Occupation: Pattern-maker, Darlington Forge Company
Regiment:	5th Durham Light Infantry

First World War - Roll of Honour
(from Darlington Library) - extract:
Arthur Dinsdale, 70 Vancouver Street, Pte. Yorkshire Dragoons
E. Dinsdale, 8 Willow Road, Pte. 1436, 5th Battn, D.L.I.
Fred Dinsdale, 10 Willow Road. Pte, 2/4 Northd. Fusiliers
W. Dinsdale, 8 Willow Road, Pte/5th D.L.I. Killed in Action, near Ypres, April 25th

Address:	Parish St Luke's; Darlington. 8 Minor Street, Darlington
Notice:	Did you receive a Notice: Yes.
Made oath to King George V	
Record for Edwin Dinsdale:	1st entry 23 Feb 1912
23 Feb 1912	Rank: Private, posted .

23 February 1912 – Edwin Dinsdale Signs Up for 4 Year Army Service

Medical Inspection Report:

Age:	17 years 2 months
Height:	5'6"
Girth when fully expanded	35"
Range of expansion	2 inches.
Vision	good
Physical development:	fair.
Certificate of approving officer:	5th battn Durham Light Infantry
Signed	29 Feb 1912 E L Hughes, Captain
7 Dec 1912 to 21 Jul 1913	Captain E L Hughes
5 Aug 1914-28 Nov 1914	
25 May 1915	Transferred
	Private 5th Reserves, DLI
29 May 1915	Private
1915	Edwin's own letter says he left for France at Xmas 1915.

---

[44] Durham Light Infantry Records and military records from the Public Record Office

EDWIN'S LETTER

The following copy of a letter written by Edwin has no date on it, but he signs it with the rank Private and there is reference to him leaving Darlington for France in Christmas 1915, so – since he was appointed Lance-Corporal in 1917, the letter must date from April 1916 to Dec 1917[45]:

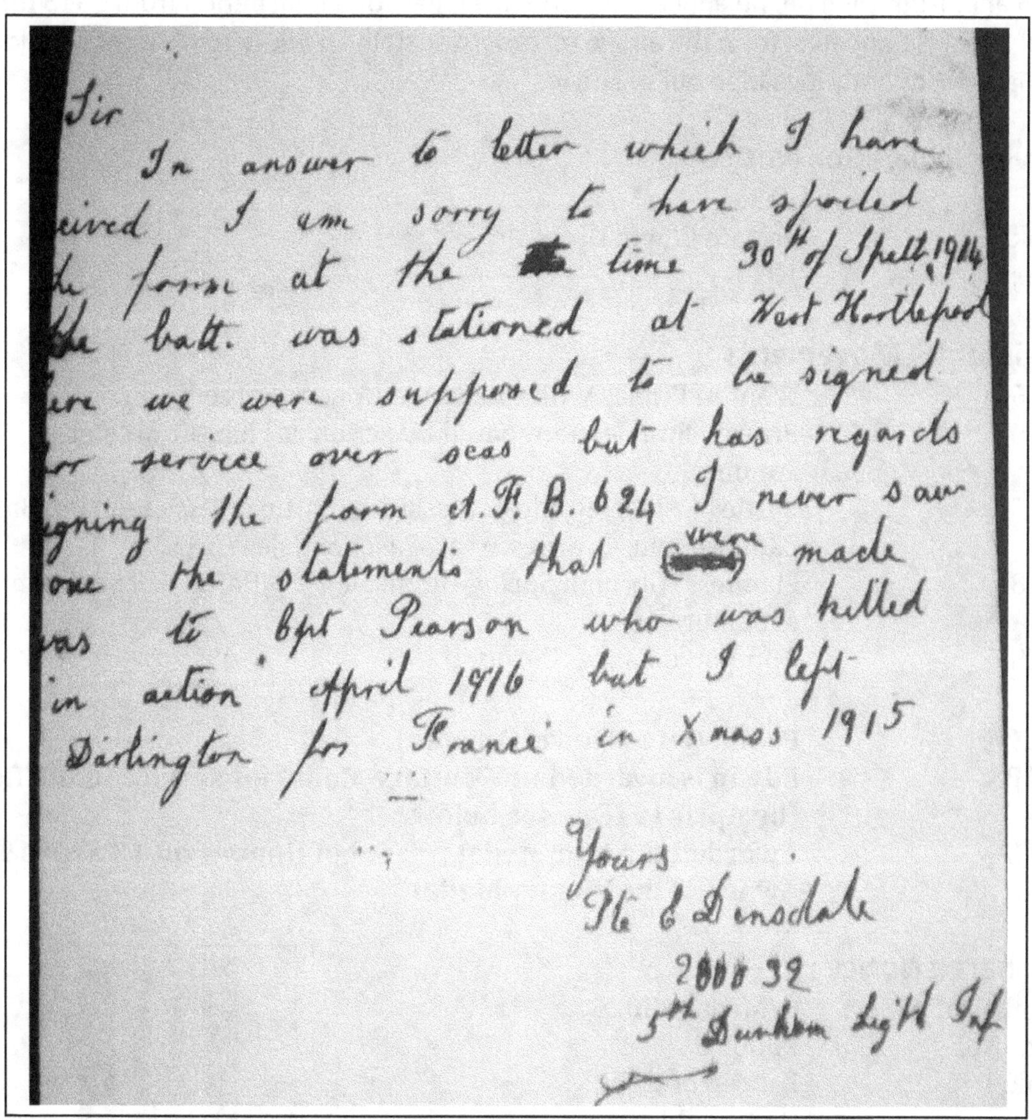

Letter reads:

Sir,

In answer to letter which I have received, I am sorry to have spoiled the form - at the time 30th September 1914 the battn. was stationed at West Hartlepool where we were supposed to be signed up for service overseas but [h]as regards signing the form A.F.B.624, I never saw one - the statements that were made was to Sgt Pearson, who was killed in action April 1916 but I left Darlington for France in Xmas 1915.

Yours Pte E. Dinsdale 280032,
5th Durham Light Infantry.

---

[45] Date of appointment as Lance-Corporal.

Military History:

Edwin's regimental movements from 1912 to 1914 were home-based, probably at training camps, then again from 1914 to 1916. 1916 would have been the end of his initial 4 years enlistment which began in 1912, but his service continues after this time for a further two years. As we have seen in Edwin's own letter, he describes being sent overseas at Christmas 1915 and, from then on, he appears to serve overseas for a long period from 1916 through to April 1918. He appears, from the above record, to sustain an injury to his right shoulder in 1918 and is subsequently invalided out of service.

Service Obligation Notice

Service:	1436
Rank:	Private Edwin Dinsdale
Date:	1917

Regiment's Movements

1915	Went to France with the Expeditionary Force
1916	Picardy France -dominated by action at Flers-Courcelette (The Somme).
1917	Battle of Arras; Battle of Messines; Battle of Paschendale; Battle of Cambrai; plus Scarpe, Arras, Paschendale, Ypres.
1918	Flanders (German Spring Offensive); 2nd Battle of The Somme; Battle of Sambre
1918	Appointed Lance- Corporal
1917	**Promoted to Lance-Corporal**
1918	**Edwin is awarded the Military Medal for service in the field (by April 1918) – see below**
1918	**Awarded the War Medal (Medal of Honour on 13 Sept 1918)**
1918	**Awarded the Victory Medal**

Discharge Notice

Number of paper:	C/Medals/3026
Regtl No.:	200032
Rank:	Lance Corporal
Regiment;	Durham LI
Awarded:	Military Medal (see right)
Address:	16 Newfoundland, Darlington

Invalid Notice

Service no:	200032, Lance Corporal
Division:	5th batt Durham Light Infantry
Date:	4 October 1918

Ministry of Pensions

Date:	30 Oct 1919

Rank:	13th battalion dli pte 200032 (1436)
	13th D. Durham LI
	23 Dec 1915
	17 dec 1917
	2 Apr 1917 –1 Apr 1918
1 May 1918	Appointed to a post I don't get paid for.
Pension:	13 Sept from 12 Oct 1918 ?? to be reviewed 32 weeks.
2 Apr 1918:	73rd Chapel Discharged.
11 Oct 1918	Private (rank) 11.10.98.
Father:	Edwin Dinsdale. Stapleton, Darlington

Medals

15 Nov 1918 War Badge and Certificate awarded to Edwin Dinsdale, service no.
200032. Address: Stapleton, Nr Darlington, awarded on 13 Nov 1918.

Lance-Corporal

Edwin was appointed Lance-Corporal in 1918 which is the rank between Private and Corporal and is the lowest rank of non-commissioned officers. During the Napoleonic Wars, the term "chosen men" was used and became a precursor to the rank.

HOME GUARD SERVICE (WWII)

Edwin was long past fighting age at the commencement of World War II, but he enrolls for the Local Defence Volunteer force on 2nd September 1940[46]. The Local Defence Volunteers (LDV) had only been formed four months before Edwin joined. Some, jokingly, referred to them, from the LDV initials, as "Look, Duck and Vanish" as their original purpose was to look out for airborne landings. They were unpaid adult volunteers who became part-time soldiers. They were renamed later after a speech by Churchill in which he called them "The Home Guard".

With the arrival of the German army in the spring of 1940 at the Channel, there were real fears of invasion and the Home Guard were put in place as a front line, to buy time for the professional army to be deployed to engage the enemy. Bombs were dropped on Darlington during WWII but not too many. The duties of the Home Guard (Dad's Army) were varied, ranging from Air Raid Wardens, Fire Wardens - ready to extinguish incendiary bombs, defending factories engaged in essential war-time activities, checking people's identity cards etc.

In his Last Will and Testament, Edwin Dinsdale (Jnr) makes reference to his Albert Hill Pension - Albert Hill being the location of the Darlington Forge Company and that he spent the happiest days of his working life there. It is known that there was a man called Thomas Summerson who gave his name to the Darlington, Albert Hill, Summerson's Home Guard. Essentially this was the Home Guard detachment of the Darlington Forge Company, of which Edwin was no doubt a member, which was under the leadership of Lieutenant W. Miller.

Edwin remained with The Home Guard, whose numbers had increased to one million, throughout its existence until it was disbanded on 31st December 1945. He died less than five months later, after he had lost all his hair due to cancer treatment but, a few weeks before he died, he wrote his Will in an informal style - not mentioning an executor ....

---

[46] National Archives, Kew: Form of Enrolment in the Local Defence Volunteers.

LAST WILL AND TESTAMENT

I, EDWIN DINSDALE, hereby declare that this i[s] my Last Will and Testimony and I wish to turn money and effect[s] over to my wife Edith Annie Dinsdale, 16 Hundens Lane East who has been a good pal to me during my spell of married [marriage]. Also I like to thank all neighbour[s] and relatives for their kindness through illness and the workmen or staff of the Darlington Forge Company where I spent the happiest time of my working life.

Items of money include War Loans invested through the Disabled Pension which been in since 1937, mature 1947. Money due from the Darlington Forge Company, Albert Hill Darlington Superannuation Fund, also War loans invested through the War Savings.

Witness Signature E Dinsdale

Signed Arnold Dinsdale   Douglas R Middleton
Stapleton   Mar. 30th 1946.
Affidavit of due execution filed.

"On the 24th August 1946 administration with this will of the estate of the testator was granted at Durham ....."

Now follows details of Edwin's wife, Edith Annie Middleton and their family.

Marriage and Children

After the end of the First World War, when Edwin has completed his military service, he marries Edith Annie Middleton in 1919 and they have six children (5 girls and a boy). Edwin was strict with the girls, not allowing them to wear make-up, or be out after 10 pm.[47]

The following pages are about Edith initially and then describes the lives of the six children they had.

EDITH ANN MIDDLETON 1899-1972

EDITH ANN[7] MIDDLETON *(JOHN CHAPMAN[6], HANNAH[5], THOMAS[4], MARK[3], JOHN[2], JOHN[1]* was born September 24, 1899 in Cotherstone, Yorkshire, and died 1972 in Darlington. She married (1) EDWIN DINSDALE. He was born 1896, and died 1946. She married (2) ARNOLD DINSDALE.

Children of EDITH MIDDLETON and EDWIN DINSDALE are:

    i.   ELSIE[6] DINSDALE, b. 1919; d. 1984.
   ii.   LAURA DINSDALE, b. 1921, Darlington; d. 1997, Derby.
  iii.   MARJORIE ELEANOR DINSDALE, b. 1923; d. 1988.
  iv.   MAURICE DINSDALE, b. 1923, Darlington; d. 1993, Darlington.
   v.   JOYCE DINSDALE, b. 1928, Darlington; d. 1972, Darlington.
  vi.   MAUREEN DINSDALE, b. 1931; d. 2002.

Picture right …
Edith Ann Middleton taken about 1915
when she would be about 16 yrs old

---

[47] According to Mrs Robert Cornforth (whose husband was grandson of Arnold Dinsdale 1887-1953).

Edith unites the Dinsdales and Middleton when she marries Edwin Dinsdale in 1919 and they have a family. After Edwin's death, she marries his brother Arnold. All her children are from her first marriage to Edwin.

Right: Edith again (on the right)
with a friend or work colleague.

The picture may date from around 1918 when it looks
as if both girls they were factory workers –
perhaps doing munitions work for WWI

Picture supplied by Moira Hollis (grand-daughter)
(daughter of Elsie Dinsdale)

Marriage to Edwin Dinsdale in 1919:

Taken in 1922, pictured right is
Edith (aged 23), Edwin (aged 27)
and youngest children;
Elsie (aged 3 yrs) and Laura (age 1)

Picture courtesy of Roslyn Semple
(grand-daughter)

Marriage to Arnold Dinsdale in 1947:

ARNOLD DINSDALE
(1888-1953)
and EDITH ANNIE
MIDDLETON (1899-1972)

After the death of her first husband
in 1946, one year later
Edith marries his brother Arnold ...

But, Arnold only lives until 1953.
And so Edith is widowed for a second time
from a DINSDALE ...

(Arnold had a prosthetic right hand)
He kept pigs on a piece of land near the
family home and worked as a plumber.

Picture courtesy of Pauline BATTY

Thirdly (and last), Edith "marries" Harry Dunn (Pop) in 1955. However, in the fullness of time,
 it turned out to be not legally valid, as he was already married with a living wife. Edith Annie was close
to Arnold's family and, even though they were only married for five years before his death, she makes
bequests to Arnold's children in her Will.

LAST WILL AND TESTAMENT

This is the Last Will of me EDITH ANNIE DINSDALE of 34 Kirkstall Crescent Darlington in the County of
Durham widow made this Twelfth day of August One Thousand Nine Hundred and Fifty Eight.
I APPOINT my brother Douglas Middleton and my sister Mary Middleton (hereinafter called my
Trustees) Executors and Trustees of this my Will. I BEQUEATH to my stepson Walter Dinsdale a legacy of
Five Pounds. I BEQUEATH my shares in Tees Side Farmers to my stepson Eric Dinsdale and my
stepdaughter Irene Dinsdale in equal shares absolutely. I GIVE all my estate both real and person not
otherwise disposed of by this my Will unto my Trustees upon trust to sell the same (with power to
postpone sale) and out of the moneys to arise from such sale and my ready money to pay my funeral,
testamentary expenses legacy and debts and divide the residue between all my children in equal shares
PROVIDED that if any child of mine shall die in my lifetime leaving issue living at my decease and who
attain twenty one years then such issue shall take and if more than one equally between them the share
in my residuary estate his her or their parent would have taken if such parent had survived me. I
REVOKE all Wills at any time heretofore made by me.

IN WITNESS whereof I have hereunto set my hand the day and year first above written.
Signed Edith Annie Dinsdale

SIGNED by the said Edith Annie Dinsdale as her last Will in the presence of us present at the same time who at her request in her presence and in the presence of each other we have hereunto subscribed our names as witnesses.

M James -   Clerks to Messrs Clayhills Lucas & Co., Solicitors, Darlington
D Bower -

It is curious that Edith Annie refers to herself as "Dinsdale" in her Will which was drawn up in 1958 because, in fact, she had married for a third time in 1955 to Harry Dunn. Perhaps she had a premonition of what was to transpire many years later - as mentioned elsewhere - Harry Dunn was not, in fact, free to marry - already having a living wife. Edith leaves specific bequests to her second husband's family - her step-children: to all three of Arnold's children: Eric, Irene and Walter Dinsdale, with the bulk of her estate to be sold off and divided equally between her own children.

Edith dies on 17th May 1972 and probate is granted on 20th June 1972 on an estate worth £841.09 (net £732.92) to the Executor Douglas Raymond Middleton of 22 Oaklands Terrace, Darlington. Probate granted by the High Court, district probate Newcastle upon Tyne.

Edith died in 1972 and is buried
with her first husband Edwin ....

Right: Two of Edwin & Edith's
Grandchildren:
Pauline BATTY and Graham PROUDLER
At the grave of Edwin & Edith Dinsdale

Taken July 2009

Edith's second husband, Arnold DINSDALE, is buried at the same cemetery in Darlington, along with his first wife ...

CHILDREN OF EDWIN DINSDALE AND EDITH MIDDLETON

Left: Maurice Edwin DINSDALE (1923-93) and right: Marjorie Eleanor DINSDALE (1923-88)

Edwin and Edith had one son and five daughters – here is mum with five daughters:
Left to right: Laura, Elsie, (Mum=Edith Ann), Marjorie, Maureen (head shot only) and Joyce.
Taken at Moira's wedding (grand-daughter) on 26th August 1967.
Picture supplied by Pauline BATTY

ELSIE DINSDALE & FAMILY
(1919-1984)

Generation No. 9

ELSIE[9] DINSDALE *(EDWIN[8], EDWIN[7], COLLINGWOOD[6], JAMES[5], JOSEPH[4], JOHN[3], JOSEPH[2], THOMAS[1])* was born October 6, 1919 in Darlington, and died December 1984 in Darlington. She married WILLIAM HENRY BLADES October 1939 in Darlington. He was born May 6, 1917 in Gateshead and died February 19, 1999 in Darlington.

Children of ELSIE DINSDALE and WILLIAM BLADES are:
112.   i.   MALCOLM[10] BLADES, b. April 28, 1947, Darlington.
113.   ii.   MOIRA PATRICIA BLADES, b. August 1, 1950.

Elsie above left, and right with husband Harry BLADES (taken on wedding day) October 1939. It is thought that Elsie worked at a Chemicals Factory in Darlington at some point.
Same couple, below, with a message from Elsie on her picture to Harry "God be with you till we meet again Harry, I love you forever, Yours Elsie. (Picture supplied by Moira Hollis – their daughter)

LAURA DINSDALE
(1921-1997)

Generation No. 9

LAURA[9] DINSDALE (*EDWIN[8], EDWIN[7], COLLINGWOOD[6], JAMES[5], JOSEPH[4], JOHN[3], JOSEPH[2], THOMAS[1]*) was born February 11, 1921 in Darlington, and died January 23, 1997 in Derby. She married (1) STANLEY QUINTIN November 1942 in Darlington. He was born February 14, 1920 in Edmonton, London, and died October 1997 in Enfield, Middlesex. She married (2) JOHN WILLIAM PROUDLER March 1948 in Derby. He was born December 15, 1923 in Derby, and died August 2011 in Derby.

JOHN WILLIAM PROUDLER: Died of asbestosis (life-long worker at Derby Loco Works, British Rail)

Children of LAURA DINSDALE and JOHN PROUDLER are:
- i.   MICHAEL[10] PROUDLER, b. December 23, 1945, Derby, m. Diane. Daughter Jennifer.
- ii. GRAHAM JOHN PROUDLER, b. July 11, 1949, Derby; m. KAREN MCLEAN, July 4, 1983, Derby

Laura, above in WWII military uniform and right (in her wedding dress from her first marriage to Stanley Quentin in Darlington in 1942 at St John's Church). It was said by a guest at this wedding (who shall remain nameless), that Laura slapped the groom across the face at the reception![48]

---

[48] Same person remembers Laura coming home to Darlington in her war-time uniform, on leave.

Left: Laura married second husband John William PROUDLER (1923-2011) in 1948 Derby where they lived.

John (Jack) died in 2011 of asbestosis caused by his life-time working at British Rail. Jack and Laura divorced in the 1980s but neither remarried. Laura moved to Darlington for some years before finally returning to Derby where she diedin 1997.

Son Michael was born 1945 and Graham 1949.

 Laura used to tell a story about being chased down Vale Street in Derby, during the Second World War, by a Nazi plane which was shooting at her. She hid in what she called Scattergood's entry (a house across the road from her home at the time), and son Graham recalls being shown the bullet holes in the building many years later. As part of the Derby Museum's Millennium Celebrations, the following news article was printed which confirms Laura's story ....

"NEWS IN BRIEF:
CIVILIANS SHOT BY ENEMY AIRCRAFT Monday 27th July 1942

Twenty-two civilians were killed and many more injured in a terrifying attack by a lone enemy aircraft today. At 7.50 am the Dornier 217 skimmed the roof tops of Rolls-Royce with bomb doors open and machine guns blazing. Two bombs caused considerable damage to stores, workshops and houses opposite the works.

The aircraft then turned its attention to Osmaston Road and surrounding streets where it gunned down workers. It then flew towards Friar Gate area where the Babbington Lane barrage balloon was shot down and a bus in Slack Lane machine-gunned".

Laura, dressed in her army uniform, was spotted by the plane and shot at. Her location would have been right on the plane's path, after leaving Rolls Royce, it would have flown over Vale Street on its way to Friar Gate. Rolls Royce was producing the Merlin engine at the time, which powered the Hurricane and Spitfire aircraft, but this was the only German aircraft to ever successfully hit the Rolls Royce factory throughout World War II. Of the four bombs it dropped, one hit the factory and the other three hit residential houses and shops, causing the biggest loss of life in Derby during the War.

MARJORIE ELEANOR DINSDALE
(1923-1988)

Generation No.9

MARJORIE ELEANOR[9] DINSDALE *(EDWIN[8], EDWIN[7], COLLINGWOOD[6], JAMES[5], JOSEPH[4], JOHN[3], JOSEPH[2], THOMAS[1])* was born July 23, 1923 in Darlington, and died June 1988 in Darlington. She married (1) JOHN MARSHALL ANDREW June 2, 1941 in Darlington. He was born 1918, and died January 1944 in Darlington. She married (2) FRANK PECKITT June 2, 1945 in St Johns Church, Darlington. He was born July 15, 1923 in Howgrave, Yorkshire, and died June 1979 in Darlington.

More About MARJORIE ELEANOR DINSDALE: Notes2: Address at marriage 24 Wycombe Street, Darlington. Sister Laura was a witness at her first marriage to John M Andrew. Nts: Twin (with Maurice). Buried West Cemetery, Darlington

More About JOHN MARSHALL ANDREW: Notes Died of throat cancer Occupation: Steelworker

Child of MARJORIE DINSDALE and JOHN ANDREW is:
115. i.JOHN EDWIN[10] ANDREW, b. December 13, 1941.

Child of MARJORIE DINSDALE and FRANK PECKITT is:
116. ii.PAULINE[10] PECKITT, b. January 5, 1946, Greenbank Hospital, Darlington.

Wedding of **Marjorie Eleanor DINSDALE** to Frank Peckitt 2 June 1945 at Darlington

MARJORIE ELEANOR DINSDALE was cremated and her remains were placed with those of her husband, Frank Peckitt, at the Remembrance Garden at Darlington Cemetery.

JOYCE MARY DINSDALE
(1928-1972)

Generation No. 9

JOYCE[9] DINSDALE *(EDWIN[8], EDWIN[7], COLLINGWOOD[6], JAMES[5], JOSEPH[4], JOHN[3], JOSEPH[2], THOMAS[1])* was born July 15, 1928 in Darlington, and died June 1972 in Darlington. She married HARRY HARBURN August 1952 in Darlington. He was born September 21, 1924 in Darlington, and died May 2006 in Darlington.

Child of JOYCE DINSDALE and HARRY HARBURN is:
    i.   ROSLYN[10] HARBURN, b. April 14, 1962.

Joyce (above) with Jack PROUDLER also on Her Wedding day – August 1952. *Joyce died of cancer.* She had worked as a tailoress at Alexander Workwear in Darlington at some time.

Wedding day 1952

Joyce Dinsdale's was cremated and her ashes were placed on her parents' grave.

MAUREEN DINSDALE & FAMILY
(1931-2002)

Generation 9

MAUREEN[9] DINSDALE (*EDWIN[8], EDWIN[7], COLLINGWOOD[6], JAMES[5], JOSEPH[4], JOHN[3], JOSEPH[2], THOMAS[1]*) was born February 1931 in Darlington, and died November 2002 in Darlington. She married GRAHAM ALBERT LEONARD October 1954 in Darlington. He died 2002 in Darlington.

More About MAUREEN DINSDALE: Occupation: Worked at the Darlington Forge Company prior to marriage, job unknown

More About GRAHAM ALBERT LEONARD: Served in military (possibly National Service) and was sent out to Malaya in early 1960s Occupation: After military service worked at Darlington Forge Company and later other jobs

Children of MAUREEN DINSDALE and GRAHAM LEONARD are:

    i.   BEVERLEY ANN[10] LEONARD, b. February 1955, Darlington; d. March 1955, Darlington.

   ii.   BARRY LEONARD, b. August 1956, Darlington; d. 2007, France.

  iii.   ANNETTE LEONARD, b. October 30, 1957, Darlington; m. MICHAEL JOHN BERESFORD, November 1992, Coalville, Leicester.
           More About ANNETTE LEONARD: Has a step-son (raised from 6 months of age)

   iv.   GILLIAN LEONARD, b. December 20, 1959, Darlington.

    v.   BARBARA E. LEONARD, b. June 9, 1961.

   vi.   MARTIN LEONARD, b. August 1962, Darlington.

  vii.   GRAHAM EDWIN LEONARD, b. February 1969, Darlington.

 viii.   JASON VICTOR LEONARD, b. August 1971, Darlington.

   ix.   MICHAEL LEONARD, b. February 1974, Darlington.

Maureen (1931-2002) married Graham Leonard in October 1954 and they had eight surviving children

L to R: Maureen, husband Graham Leonard & sister Marjorie Eleanor

Prior to marriage, it is thought that Maureen worked at the Darlington Forge Company - though it is unknown in what capacity.

Husband Graham Leonard was doing military service (possibly in the catering core) in the early years of their marriage and was deployed to Malaya. Following the Japanese withdrawal from that area, after their defeat in the Second World War, there was a political vacuum which the Malayan Communist Party tried to fill by engaging in violence in a guerrilla type war against the allied forces, principally the British. The term "war", however, was never used to describe the conflict - as Lloyds of London would have frozen assets/finances if the action had been termed as such, so it was referred to as an "emergency". Well, the "emergency" ended up with some 40,000 British soldiers despatched to quell the communist uprising and by the early-mid 1960s they had succeeded. Graham is thought to have asked wife Maureen to join him out in Malaya but she declined and so he ended his military career and returned to the UK. He worked in various capacities thereafter, including a time at Darlington's biggest employer, the Forge Company.

Maureen was pregnant 13 times, but miscarried on occasions, with eight children surviving. The couple die within months of each other in 2002.

Eldest daughter Annette moved away from Darlington many years ago to Donisthorpe in Leicestershire and is married with a step-son.

Maureen was cremated and a memorial to her and husband Graham Leonard is located at Edith and Edwin DINSDALE's grave –

The stone base for the above "angel statue" was made by their son Graham.

SIBLINGS OF EDWIN DINSDALE (JNR)

Brothers in Arms

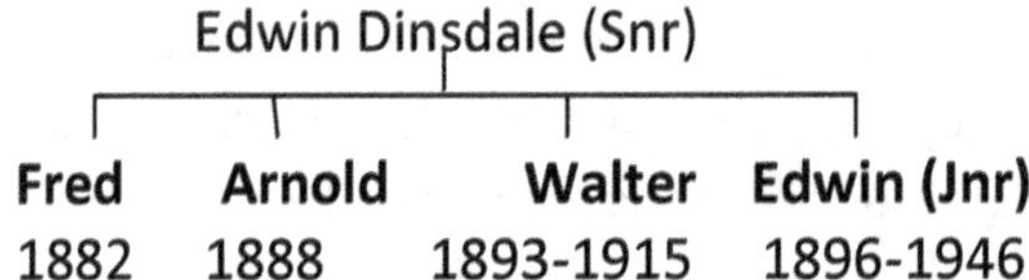

Fred Dinsdale 1882-1955 - Military Service

In 1901 Edwin's elder brother Fred is to be found as a Student Salvation Army Officer at the Congress Hall, Lynscott Road, Lower Clapton Road, Hackney, London[49]. Then by the 1911 census he is a grocer.

He also enlisted in WWI in the Northumberland Fusiliers, regiment number 204002. This regiment was formed back in 1685 and, among its nicknames were, "The Fighting Fifth", or "Wellington's Bodyguards". Some 52 battalions were deployed in the First World War and were involved in all the major campaigns. Fred was awarded the Victory Medal.

He married later in life, in 1941, to Hilda Mary Walton and they lived at 22 Gordon Crescent, Richmond, Yorkshire. There do not appear to have been any children from the marriage. Fred died on 5 February 1955 at Friargate Hospital, North Allerton, Yorks and left an estate valued at £1319 12s 7d to his widow. Hilda Mary, born 1894 in Thirsk, Yorkshire, died twenty years later in 1975.

As the eldest son, he took the lead in arranging probate when his father Edwin died in 1928.

Richmond Cemetery's Monumental Inscriptions records them both being buried there.

Arnold Dinsdale - 1887-1953

Arnold, the second eldest brother, is on the 1911 census working as a plumber. Arnold is significant in this booklet not just in his own right, but also for the fact that he became Edith Middleton's second husband, after youngest Edwin - who had been her first husband - died.

No military records have been found for Arnold from the First World War but it is known that, at some point, he had a prosthetic arm fitted. It is visible in 1948 in his wedding photographs to Edith Middleton.

His first marriage took place in 1913 in Darlington to Margaret Lewins and they had three children: Eric 1914-2006, Irene 1916-1981 and Walter Collingwood 1919-1991. There are descendants living today from all three of these children who have helped with information for this research.

---

[49] 1901 census.

Arnold had a bungalow built in the grounds of his father's house in Stapleton according to his grandson Peter Staley Dinsdale. At son Eric's wedding, Arnold lists his occupation again as plumber.

Chronology - Arnold

1887	Born in Eckington, Derbyshire
1911	On 1911 census working as a plumber
1913	Marries Margaret Lewins, house built at Stapleton next to parents
1914	Eldest son Eric is born
1916	Daughter Irene is born
1919	Youngest son Walter Collingwood is born
1939	Son Eric marries Betty Hodgson at St Matthews in Darlington
1939	Occupation still plumber (son's wedding certificate)
1939	Address: The Bungalow, Stapleton (built in his father's garden)
1947	Wife Margaret dies
1948	Marries Edith Middleton and lives at her home
1953	Dies

Walter Dinsdale 1893-1915 - Military Service

Edwin's elder brother Walter also served in the First World War but was Killed in Action at Ypres ....

DINSDALE, WALTER

Rank:	Private
Service No:	2423
Date of Death:	26/04/1915
Age:	30
Regiment/Service:	Durham Light Infantry 1st/5th Bn.
Panel Reference	Panel 36 and 38.
Memorial	YPRES (MENIN GATE) MEMORIAL

ADDITIONAL INFORMATION:

Son of Mr. and Mrs. Dinsdale, of Stapleton Village, Darlington.

Record from the Commonwealth War Graves site.

The age is incorrectly recorded as Walter was 22 years old at death. He was awarded the Victory Medal, the British Medal and The Star[50]. Theatre of War: France 1914-15 Campaign. 1/5th Btn Durham Light Infantry. Rank Pte 2423.

Walter's full service record does not appear to have survived but it is thought that he was unmarried at the time of his death. Walter's date of death is 26th April 1915 and, on that day, his 1st/5th Battalion were engaged in the 2nd Battle of Ypres:-
26 April 1915 - Battle of Ypres, 50th (Northumbrian) Division prevented capture of the city. 2nd Battalion at Ypres Canal until July.

70,000 allied soldiers dead or wounded against 30,000 German soldiers - result "stalemate".

Walter's name is on the War Memorial at Darlington Hospital.

Clara Ann Dinsdale 1881-1952

Edwin's sister Clara Ann is born in 1881 in Eckington, Derbyshire/S. Yorkshire area. She marries Frederick Sydney Grieveson in 1903 at Darlington.

Son Edwin Collingwood G.G. Dinsdale is born 1908 and immediately the family set sail for America where they are to be found on the 1910 census at 104 Lagrange Township, Lorain in Ohio. Lorain is located in north-eastern Ohio on Lake Erie about thirty miles west of Cleveland. Fred is working as a Section Head for the 4C Rail Road Company - the census shows their immigration year to be 1909 and actually states their infant son Edwin to have been born in Ohio. They are living in a rented house on a farm - probably this would be temporary accommodation which would be erected from site to site as the progress of the railway build moved.   The family stay in Ohio for about ten years and Fred is recorded on the 1918 Ohio Draft WWI papers, before they return to Darlington by 1919. It is as well that they did leave at this time as, just a few years later in 1924, a tornado devastates the area. The family remain in Darlington until Fred's early death in 1925. Son Edwin (1908-84) remains in Darlington and marries in 1950 to Alice Cleminson but they have no children.

Edith Dinsdale (nee Middleton) 1899-1972,

in later years ....

Picture supplied by Jack PROUDLER

---

[50] Victory Medal Roll 0/1/103 B5, page 770; British Medal Roll 0/1/103 B5 page 770, The Star Medal Roll 10/1/6B page 221.

Census Returns - Collingwood Dinsdale

1841 Census

Parish: Thornton Curtis, Yarborough Hundred, Lincolnshire. Registration District Glanford Brigg. Address: *Thornton, Thornton Curtis, Burnham, Lincs.* Household Members: William Story, age 60 occupation farmer, John Story, age 35, Rebecca Story, age 30, John Harmston, age 15, Mary Brocklesby, age 20. Thomas Sinderson, age 20. Collingwood Dinsdale, age 12 (born 1829, born Lincoln). Piece 646, book 17, folio 8, page 9.

1851 Census - *spelt Dindsdale*

Parish: Keelby, Lincolnshire Household Members: John Dean, age 43, (head). Mary Dean, age 20, wife. George Dean, age 2, son. Collingwood Dinsdale, age 22, occupation labourer (brother), born East Halton, Lincs. Lydia Dinsdale, age 63, widowed, mother in law. Piece 2114, folio 20, page 10.

1861 Census

Parish: Keelby, Lincolnshire. Registration District Caistor. Household Members: Collingwood Dinsdale, age 32, (head) occupation agricultural labourer, Ann Clara, age 31 (wife). James Wm Dinsdale, age 8. Edwin Dinsdale, age 6. Henry Collingwood. Dinsdale, age 4. (Piece 2393, folio 71, page 13)

1871 Census - *spelt Dunsdale*

Parish Letwell, Nottingham. Registration District Worksop (sub district Carlton). Address: *Village Street, Letwell.* Household Members: Collingwood Dinsdale, age 42 occupation farm labourer, Ann Clara age 41, Harry, age 14, Shearman, age 9 and Mary, age 6. Piece 3461, folio 12, page 15.

1881 Census

Parish: Eckington, Derbyshire. Street Address: *Mosbro Hill Cemetery Lodge, Mill Lane, Eckington.* Household Members: Collingwood Dinsdale, age 57, born Roxby, Lincoln. Occupation Sexton (Church Officer). Ann Clara Dinsdale, age 50, wife. Alfred Dinsdale, age 9, son. Frances Mary Dinsdale, age 16 (daughter). Clara Ann Dinsdale, age 3. (grand-daughter - daughter of Robert John born 1852). Piece 3440, folio 80, page 3.

1891 Census

Parish, Eckington, Derbyshire . Street Address: *Mosbro Hill Cemetery Lodge, Mill Lane, Eckington.* Household Members: Collingwood Dinsdale, age 64, born Roxby, Lincolnshire. Clara Ann Dinsdale, age 63. (wife) Alfred, age 19 (son). Clara Ann, age 13 (daughter). Gertrude, age 9 (daughter) and Thomas Edginton, age 74.

1901

Parish, Eckington, Derbyshire. Address: *9 Littlemoor, Eckington.* Household Members: George H Norman (head) and wife Clara Ann (Collingwood's grand-daughter) Robert Collingwood Norman (son), John Frederick Norman (son) and Collingwood Dinsdale, occupation general labourer. Piece 3258, folio 21, page 33.

1911 Census

Parish: Eccleshall Bierlow, Sheffield. Address *10 Pisgah House Road, Broomhill, Sheffield.* Household Members: Robert John Dinsdale, age 59 (head) - son of Collingwood Dinsdale, Rebecca Dinsdale (wife), age 53, Collingwood Dinsdale, age 81 (widowed), Gertrude Dinsdale, age 29. Robert Dinsdale, age 23. Dorothy Dinsdale, age 13. Rosa Alice Dinsdale, age 10. Margaret Dinsdale, age 6. Piece 27748 ref. **RG14PN27748 RG78PN1588 RD509 SD2 ED28 SN107.**

Appendix 1 - Census Returns for Collingwood Dinsdale

Census Returns - Edwin Dinsdale (Snr)

1861 Census - Caistor "all that part of the parish of Keelby lying to the north of Grimsby Road leaving the church to the east".

Collingwood Dinsdale, age 32, occupation agricultural labourer, born Halton, Lincs

Ann Clara, wife, age 31, b. 1830 in Keelby, James Wm, son, age 8, b. 1853, scholar, born Keelby

Edwin, son, age 6, b. 1855, born Keelby, Henry Collingwood, age 2, b. 1859, born Keelby

Piece 2393, folio 71, page 13, Caistor, Keelby, Lincs

1871 Census, Hanover Street, Upper, Ecclesall Bierlow, Sheffield

Chas Josh Muddiman, age 35, b. 1836 Northampton, Mary Ann Muddiman, age 28, b. 1843, Nottingham, Edwin Dinsdale, servant, age 16, b. 1855, Yorkshire.

Piece 3670, folio 160, page 6.

1881 48 Church Row, Eckington

Edwin Dinsdale, married age 26, b. 1855, occupation coal man, born Keelby, Lincs

Eleanor Dinsdale, age 26, b. 1855, born Beckingham, Nottingham

Eleanor Dinsdale, age 3, b. 1878, born Beckingham, Nottingham

Clara Ann Dinsdale, age 0, b. 1881, Beckingham, Nottingham. Piece 3440, folio 82, page 8.

1891 19 Alliance Street, Darlington

Edwin Dinsdale age 36, b. 1855, occupation labourer, gas works. Born Keelby, Lincs

Eleanor Dinsdale, age 36, born Beckingham, Notts

Eleanor Dinsdale, age 13, b. 1878, scholar, born Beckingham, Notts

Clara A. Dinsdale, age 10, b. 1881, scholar born Beckingham, Notts

Fred Dinsdale, age 9, b. 1882, scholar, born Eckington

Arnold Dinsdale, age 3, b. 1888, born Eckington

Lydia Dinsdale, age 2, b. 1889, born Eckington

John C. Dinsdale, age 0, b. 1891, born Darlington. Piece 4042, folio 116, page 51.

1901 Census 1522 Walker Road, Byker, Newcastle

Edwin Dinsdale, age 43, boarder. Occupation general labourer

Piece 4792 folio 99, page 31.

1911 Census

Edwin Dinsdale, age 55 years, born Keelby, Lincs. Address: 8 Minor Street, Darlington, status married.
Occupation, Labourer, Foundry. Registration District 543, Darlington. Piece 29514

Household Members:- Edwin Dinsdale, head, married, age 55, labourer foundry, born Keelby Lincs

Eleanor Dinsdale, wife, married, age 55, born Beckingham, Notts

Eleanor Dinsdale, daughter, married, age 32 years, female

Clara Ann Dinsdale, daughter, single, age 30 years, female

Fred Dinsdale, son, single, age 29 years, male

Arnold Dinsdale, male, age 24, occupation plumber, born Eckington, Derbyshire

Lydia Dinsdale, daughter, female, age 22, born Eckington, Derbyshire

Walter Dinsdale, son, male, age 18 labourer in foundry, born Darlington, Durham

Edwin Dinsdale, son, male, age 14, errand boy milk, born Darlington, Durham

Anthony O'Connor, grandson, male, age 10, school, born Langley Moor, Durham

Edwin O'Connor, grandson, male, age 8, born Langley Moor, Durham.

Appendix 2 - Census Returns for Edwin Dinsdale Snr